Noir

Peter Straughan

Methuen Drama

Published by Methuen Drama

1 3 5 7 9 10 8 6 4 2

First published in 2002 by
Methuen Publishing Limited

A CIP catalogue record is available from the British Library

ISBN 0 413 77271 3

Typeset by SX Composing DTP, Rayleigh, Essex
Printed and bound in Great Britain by
Cox & Wyman Ltd, Reading, Berkshire

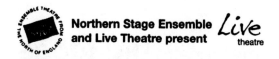

Northern Stage Ensemble and Live Theatre present *Live* theatre

NOIR

A little knowledge is a dangerous thing.

Written by Peter Straughan

Cast in order of appearance

Mark Calvert Reverend Lang
Maggie Norris Ruth Hollis
Tracy Gillman Waitress/Dr Meyers/Croupier/a GP
Michael Hodgson Ray Keyes
Deka Walmsley George Hollis
Jim Kitson Howard Day
Joe Caffrey Morris Talman
Jill Halfpenny Alison Day
Peter Peverley Customer/various roles
Mark Lloyd Barber/various roles

Director Max Roberts
Production Design Imogen Cloët
Lighting Design Malcolm Rippeth
Music Jim Kitson
AV and Sound Design Rob Brown
Fight Direction Richard Ryan

**Performed at Newcastle Playhouse
from 8-25 May 2002**

Live theatre small theatre **big ideas**

Live Theatre explores ideas in new writing. We believe in relationships with writers and in the development of new writing. We are passionate about transforming these ideas into performance of the highest quality for stage and also for radio, film and television.

Live Theatre has its roots in the identity of the North of England creating and presenting work that is challenging, popular and of relevance to all.

Our venue is accessible and friendly, providing an arts programme that is unique to Newcastle and the North East. We engage all sectors of the community as participants and audiences. Live Theatre seeks to deliver this programme through a series of regional, national and international partnerships.

history

Live Theatre Company was formed in 1973. It has developed a strong national reputation for developing and nurturing new writing in the north of England. Over the last 28 years the company has forged relationships with a number of writers including CP Taylor, Sid Chaplin, Tom Hadaway, Leonard Barras, Alan Plater, and more recently Peter Flannery, Michael Chaplin, Karin Young, Lee Hall, Peter Straughan, Julia Darling and Sean O'Brien. Many well known actors have an association with Live Theatre including Tim Healey, who was one of the company's founder members, Denise Welch and Robson Green who gives substantial financial support to Live Lines - Live Theatre's training and outreach department.

The company has been based in premises on Newcastle's quayside since 1982. Over the last 20 years, the company's premises have grown to accommodate a theatre space, rehearsal room, company offices, café-bar and restaurant.

radio, television and film

As well as presenting work for the stage, Live Theatre has forged partnerships with broadcast media and film. In the last year, Live was involved in the following projects;

May 2001 Radio 3 recorded *Laughter When We're Dead*, a play written by Sean O'Brien and commissioned and produced by Live Theatre in 2000.

July 2001 Live Theatre's Artistic Director, Max Roberts, made his TV directorial debut with a short TV drama by Peter Straughan, called *Waiters*, which was broadcast to the Tyne Tees, Yorkshire and Granada television regions.

Summer 2001 Live acted as Production Associates on a new film project with Assassin Films. *The One & Only*, written by Peter Flannery was given script development support by Live in 2000.

October 2001 BBC announced its investment in Live Theatre as part of *Northern Exposure*, to plan a two year programme of support and events for writers in the region. This includes a development project to create new drama product for BBC television.

December 2001 BBC Radio 4 broadcast three new plays about philosophers, live from the theatre. The plays were written by Sean O'Brien and Julia Darling (Live's current Writers In Residence) and Peter Straughan.

new writing

Live Theatre is currently involved in partnerships for new writing projects with *Hampstead Theatre*, the *Elements Drama Initiative County Durham*, *The Royal Shakespeare Company* and the *BBC*. A production of Lee Hall's *Cooking With Elvis*, directed by Max Roberts, completed a 15-week number 1 national tour in December 2001. Peter Straughan's *Bones*, a co-production with Hampstead Theatre has just completed critically acclaimed runs in both Newcastle and London .

The company has recently gained significant new investment from its regular stakeholders to invest in its creative programme. The principle focus of these new resources is into the development of writers and new writing. This will enable Live Theatre to stage more productions, to make more commissions, and to provide strategies and services for developing writing talent regionally and nationally.

education & participation

In 1998, the company set up an education, training and outreach department, Live Lines. This department, co-ordinates the activities of the Live Youth Theatre which has over 200 current members, Live Wires, the over 50s writing and performance group and Live writers, a writing group for young people. This department delivers one of the largest arts participation programmes in Newcastle, with over 5000 individual training sessions annually. The department also works with a large number of partners in the community.

Live Lines is supported by Coastal Productions, Granada Media and the Northern Rock Foundation.

live theatre staff

Jim Beirne Executive Director
Max Roberts Artistic Director
Wendy Barnfather Finance & Admin Manager
Chris Durant Technical Manager
Jeremy Herrin Associate Director, New Writing
Paul James Associate Director, Live Lines
Sarah McPhail Marketing & Sales Manager
Carole Wears House Manager
Irum Ashraf Asian Arts Co-ordinator
Degna Bailey Administrator
Kath Boodhai Deputy House Manager
Sarah Clarke Press & Marketing Officer
Tearlach Duncanson Outreach Drama Worker, Live Lines
Dave Flynn Technician
Laura Lindow Resident Drama Worker, Live Lines
Catherine Moody Box Office Supervisor
Harriet Morgan Administrator, Live Lines

Live Theatre is supported by

For more information about Live Theatre or to join our mailing list call 0191 232 1232 or email info@live.org.uk

www.live.org.uk

Live Theatre 27 Broad Chare Quayside Newcastle upon Tyne NE1 3DQ

Northern Stage Ensemble

"The best of what regional theatre can do" - Lord Bragg

Northern Stage Ensemble is the largest producing theatre company in the North East of England and is based at Newcastle Playhouse and the Gulbenkian Studio. The company is one of the top ten UK producing theatres, and was recently described in The Guardian as *"an egalitarian, project-based group of artists, technicians and support staff [that] has aggressively forged a new identity for regional theatre in the 21st century."*

Northern Stage Productions

Under the inspirational leadership of Alan Lyddiard, the company has gained a reputation for visually driven, multi-media productions that succeed time and again in attracting new, young audiences. In 2001, the company was nominated for Best Theatre at the Barclay's TMA Awards. Since its creation the Northern Stage Ensemble has produced nationally acclaimed work such as George Orwell's *1984, Pandora's Box, The Adventures of Pinocchio, The Tiger's Bride* and *The Ballroom of Romance* which earned Alan Lyddiard a Barclay's TMA Award nomination for Best Director.

International Partners

Besides producing its own work Northern Stage Ensemble is dedicated to presenting the best in local, national and international theatre and to developing partnerships with companies and practitioners such as Robert Lepage, Le Styx Théâtre, Peter Brook, Alain Platel and Lev Dodin of the Maly Drama Theatre of St Petersburg. In 2001 the company hosted the UK premieres of Robert Lepage's *the far side of the moon* and Declan Donnellan's *Boris Godunov* which featured some of Russia's finest actors. At the beginning of 2002 Northern Stage was nominated for the International Theatre Institute's Award for Excellence in International Theatre which was made in recognition of the company's continuing commitment and contribution to international theatre. In May 2002 Northern Stage convened an Informal International Theatre Collaborations Meeting which brought together leading directors and producers from all over the world.

Participation

Participation is at the heart of the Ensemble's work. Every year it involves thousands of people in theatre activities both at home and on tour. Projects are both inspired by the work on stage and by the community it serves. The projects aim to provide space for participants to develop their own creativity and provoke debate about the issues raised by the work on stage.Recent projects have included *In the Blink of an Eye* - a short film about the choices teenagers face which was created with young people from Newbiggin and Blyth and *Neverland* - an under 5's drama and visual arts project developed with 3 nurseries from the West End of Newcastle.

Northern Stage also has a thriving performance group with over 100 members who have successfully staged productions in both the Playhouse and in the Gulbenkian as well as appearing in *The Ballroom of Romance* and the film footage of *1984* and *The Tiger's Bride*. Most recently the group has been involved in *Fragments*, a project inspired by the production of *Noir*.

Northern Stage Ensemble
Artistic Director Alan Lyddiard
Executive Director Caroline Routh

For further information please contact:
Northern Stage Ensemble Newcastle Playhouse Barras Bridge Newcastle upon Tyne NE1 7RH

Telephone: 0191 230 5151
Fax: 0191 261 8093
email: info@northernstage.com
website: www.northernstage.com

Northern Stage Ensemble is supported by:

Esmee Fairbairn Foundation
Calouste Gulbenkian Foundation
The Northern Rock Foundation
Readman Foundation

The Northern Stage Ensemble on the opening of Noir on 8 May 2002 is:

Francisco Alfonsin Performer
Chris Allen Technical Casual
Sharon Ayre Customer Services Assistant
Tim Bailey Capital Development Project Manager
Leanne Bell Customer Services Assistant
Lauren Bishop Marketing Officer
Bev Briggs Head of Marketing
Rob Brown Sound and AV Designer
Mark Calvert Performer
Chris Carr Administration Assistant
John Cobb Associate Director
Louisa Cockburn Usher
Chris Collett Press Officer
John Disley Deputy Front of House Manager
Frances Easter Sales & Data Manager
Alex Elliott Performer
Anna Evans Usher
Gillian Firth Fundraising Manager
Joan Gibson Housekeeper
Amy Golding Usher
Brenda Gray PA to Directors
Peter Green Production Manager
Simon Henderson Assistant Stage Manager
Rebecca Hollingsworth Performer
Colin Holman Stage Manager
Tanya Holman Wardrobe Mistress
Nicola Irvine Deputy Stage Manager
Rebecca Jackson Front of House Manager
Adel Johnson Associate Director
Gemma Kopel Usher
Jim Kitson Performer
Stacey Lamb Usher
Mark Lloyd Performer
John Lock Assistant Carpenter
Mo Lovatt Programming & Planning Co-ordinator
Jamie Lumley Assistant Carpenter
Alan Lyddiard Artistic Director
Joanne McKenna Accountant
James Mavin Technical Casual
Susan Mulholland Assistant Sales & Data Manager/School Liaison Co-ordinator
Ed Murray Usher
Neil Murray Associate Director & Designer
Tony Neilson Performer
Edmund Nickols Director of Operations
Graeme Nixon Technical Manager
Rebecca Owen Marketing Assistant
John Parrack Technical Casual
Keith Pattison Photographer
Peter Peverley Performer
Amanda Purvis Company Manager
Sarah Quinney LX Technician
Rob Reed Technical Casual
Chloe Ribbens Deputy Stage Manager
Paul Robson Technical Casual
Peter Ross Technical Casual
Caroline Routh Executive Director
Anna Scatola Wardrobe Cutter
Andrew Sharp Usher
Jill Sharp Accounts Assistant
Chris Slater Chief LX
Kylie Stark Projects Manager
Andrew Stephenson Assistant Stage Manager
Andrew Stenhouse Distributor
Holly Stewart Usher
Mick Storrie Deputy Chief Technician
Alison Stringer Head of Wardrobe
Joe Stringer Usher
Diane Thoburn Wardrobe Assistant
Kevin Tweedy Electrics Technician
Rachel Unthank Usher/Distributor
Suzanne Walker Tour Producer
Sarah Warden Usher
Sam Willis Customer Services Assistant
Alan Wood Scenic Artist
Mike Wymark Head of Workshops

board of directors

peter straughan writer

Peter has worked with Live for a number of years and was the company's Writer in Residence in 1999.

Theatre credits include; *Cold* (The Ashton Group) *The Ghost of Federico Garcia Lorca Which Can Also Be Used As A Table* (Northern Stage), *Fetish - ne1* (Live Theatre), *Rat* (Pink Pony Theatre, New York) and *A Rhyme For Orange* (winner of the 1997 North East People's Play Award) and *Bones* (Live Theatre 1999 and 2002 and Hampstead Theatre 2002).

Peter's TV drama *Waiters* for Peter Mitchell Ltd/Tyne Tees Television/Northern Production fund was broadcast in July 2001.

Radio 4 have also produced his play *When We Were Queens* and his adaptation of Andrew Motion's *Wainewright The Poisoner* and *Centurions* (co-written with Bridget O'Connor)

Peter has completed writing his first feature film, *Five Psychopaths*, for Contagious Films, who have also commissioned a second film, *The Edward Stark Trilogy*.

In radio, Peter won the Alfred Bradley Award for his adaptation of his own stage play, *The Ghost of Federico Garcia Lorca*.

max roberts director

Max is the Artistic Director of Live Theatre, Newcastle upon Tyne.

Favourite productions include; *The Long Line, Long Shadows* and *Seafarers* (Tom Hadaway), *Close The Coalhouse Door, Going Home, Shooting the Legend* and *Tales from the Backyard* (Alan Plater), *In Blackberry Time* (Alan Plater and Michael Chaplin from the stories of Sid Chaplin), *Twelve Tales of Tyneside* (Peter Flannery and others), *Northern Glory* (Phil Woods), *Laughter When We're Dead* (Sean O'Brien), *Only Joking* (Steve Chambers), *Buffalo Girls and Eggs and Basket Cases* (Karin Young) and *Cooking With Elvis* (Olivier Award Nominee - Best Comedy), *ne1* and *Wittgenstein on Tyne* (Lee Hall) and *Bones* (Peter Straughan).

cast

Joe Caffrey Morris Talman

Joe trained at LAMDA. Theatre credits include: *The Last Post, ne1,
Cabaret, Twelve Tales of Tyneside, Close the Coalhouse Door,
Bandits, Your Home in the West, The Beautiful Game* and *Kiddars
Luck* (Live Theatre), *Births, Marriages and Deaths, Beauty and the
Beast, Out of the Blue* and *Trouble Under Foot* (Northern Stage),
Studs (Hull Truck Theatre) and *Cooking With Elvis* (Live Theatre and
West End national tour).

TV credits include: *Attachments, Holby City, Hetty Wainthrop
Investigates, Badger, Byker Grove* and *Spender (BBC)*, Catherine
Cookson's *Colour Blind, Soldier Soldier, The Last Musketeer,
Ain't Misbehaving* and *Quayside* (ITV)

Radio credits include: *Spiders War, The Lower Depths,
The Newcastle Mysteries, My Uncle Freddie, Who Me?* and
Francie Nichol (BBC Radio 4)

Mark Calvert Reverend Lang

Mark is a founder member of the Northern Stage Ensemble.
He trained at Manchester Metropolitan School of Theatre and New
College Durham. For Northern Stage Ensemble his credits include:
A Clockwork Orange, Romeo in *Romeo & Juliet, You'll Have Had
Your Hole*, Tony Harrison's *V, Grimm Tales, More Grimm Tales,
The Ballroom of Romance, 1984, Glengarry Glen Ross, The Dumb
Waiter* and *Pinocchio*. He has also worked with the Contact Theatre,
Manchester and Durham Theatre Company.

Tracy Gillman Waitress/Dr Meyer/Croupier/a GP

Tracy appeared in many productions for the Tyne and Wear Theatre
Company including *Sweeny Todd* and *Strippers*. Other theatre
credits include: *Black and White Shorts* (tour); *Foreign Lands*
(Finborough Arms); *Phantom of the Opera* (Shaftesbury/Tour);
Our Country's Good (Chester Gateway); *In the Midnight Hour*
(Coventry/UK Tour); *Little Hotel on Side* (Cheltenham Everyman);
Dig Volley, Spike (Old Red Lion) and *As You Like It* (Dukes
Playhouse). On TV she has appeared in *Casualty, Cracker* and
Dangerfield. Tracy's film credits include *Skallagrigg* and *Last Days of
the Post Office*. She will also appear as Maureen the Social Worker
in the forthcoming film, *The One and Only*.

Jill Halfpenny Alison Day

Jill's TV credits include Rebecca in *Coronation Street*, *Dalziel and Pascoe*, *Peak Practice*, *Dangerfield*, *Touching Evil*, *Heartbeat*, *The Lakes*, *The Bill* and *Byker Grove*. Her theatre credits include *Studs* and *Like a Virgin* (Hull Truck Theatre); *The Sound of Music* (Sheffield Crucible); *Jumping the Waves* (Arc, Teeside) and a national tour of Lee Hall's *Cooking with Elvis*. Most recently Jill appeared in Northern Stage Ensemble's production of *1984*.

Michael Hodgson Ray Keyes

Michael's work for Live Theatre includes *Bones* (Live Theatre and Hampstead Theatre), *My Last Barmaid - ne1* (Live Theatre and Newcastle Theatre Royal), *Fetish - ne1* and *Laughter When We're Dead*. Other theatre work includes *Studs* (Hull Truck Theatre), *King Lear* (Young Vic/Tokyo Globe, Japan), *The Tower* (Almedia Theatre), *Wind in the Willows* and *The Devils Disciple* (National Theatre), *Jane Eyre* (West End) and *The Guise* (Edinburgh, Hong Kong, New York - Winner of Fringe First Award 1990).

Television credits include: *Dalziel & Pascoe*, *Without Motive II*, *The Bill* (Guest Lead), *Touching Evil* and *The Tide of Life*.

Film credits include: *The One & Only*, *Purely Belter*, *The Lowdown*, *Wonderland* and *First Knight*.

Radio credits include: *Laughter When We're Dead* (BBC Radio 3) and *Barbarians* (BBC Radio 4).

Jim Kitson Howard Day

Jim is a founder member of the Northern Stage Ensemble. For the company he has appeared in *Animal Farm*, *A Clockwork Orange*, *The Ballroom of Romance*, *The Selfish Giant*, *The Oklahoma Outlaw*, *Glengarry Glen Ross*, *Edmond* and *Pinocchio*, and the film footage for *1984* and *The Tiger's Bride*. Jim has also worked extensively with North East based companies Théâtre Sans Frontières, Cleveland Theatre Company, NTC Touring Theatre Company and Live Theatre.

Mark Lloyd Barber/various roles

Mark is a founder member of the Northern Stage Ensemble. He trained at LAMDA and first worked with Northern Stage on the Sunderland based *Journey's Project* in 1994. He has since appeared in *Animal Farm*, *A Clockwork Orange*, *Romeo & Juliet*, *Bert's Big Night Out*, *The Ballroom of Romance*, *The Selfish Giant*, *The Oklahoma Outlaw*, *Edmond*, *Glengarry Glen Ross*, *Play*, *Pinocchio* and *The Dumb Waiter*.

Maggie Norris Ruth Hollis

Maggie's theatre credits include: *Not Quite It* (Soho Theatre); *Seeds Under Stones* and *Good Copy* (West Yorkshire Playhouse); *Road to Nirvana* (Traverse Theatre); *The Miser* and *See How they Run* (Salisbury Playhouse); *Court in the Act* (Royal Exchange); *Annie and Fanny from Bolton to Rome* (Bolton Octagon); *East and Greek* (Manchester Library) and *Macbeth* (Young Vic). TV includes: *EastEnders, Casualty; Moving On; Peak Practice; Where the Heart is; Only Fools and Horses* and *Coronation Street*.

Peter Peverley Customer/various roles

Peter is a founder member of the Northern Stage Ensemble. For Northern Stage he has performed in *Twelfth Night*, *A Clockwork Orange*, *Animal Farm*, *Grimm Tales*, *More Grimm Tales*, *The Ballroom of Romance*, *The Oklahoma Outlaw*, *Edmond*, *Glengarry Glen Ross*, *Pinocchio* and *The Dumb Waiter*. Last year, he performed his one-man show about the life of North East legend, Bobby Thompson, in the Gulbenkian Studio and other venues across the region.

Deka Walmsley George Hollis

Deka's work for Live Theatre includes: *Bones* (Live Theatre and Hampstead Theatre) *ne1, Laughter When We're Dead, Some Voices, Long Shadows,* and *Tales from the Backyard*. Other theatre credits include; *Animal Farm* (Northern Stage), *Mapping The Edge* (WilsonWilson/Sheffield Crucible), 'Sammy' in *Blood Brothers* (West End) and *Cooking With Elvis* (West End).

TV credits include: *Rebus, Ticket To Ride, Our Friends in the North, Eastenders* and *Badger*.

Film credits include: *Dream On* and *Like Father.*

Deka has worked extensively for BBC Radio 3 & 4. Credits include: *Laughter When We're Dead, The Taming of the Shrew, A Midsummer Night's Dream* and *Frozen Images*.

production

Imogen Cloët Production Designer

Imogen is a freelance set and costume designer based in the North East. In 1996, she received the Arts Council Theatre Design Bursary and last year was shortlisted for the prestigious Arts Foundation Scenography Award. Theatre work: For Live Theatre: *Cooking With Elvis*, *I Cannot Tell a Lie*, and costume for *Bones* (1999) and *Falling Together*. For Northern Stage: *You'll Have Had Your Hole*, Tony Harrison's *V.* and *The Selfish Giant*. Imogen has also worked for Opera North, Welfare State International, New Writing North, Foolsyard Theatre Company, Théâtre Sans Frontières and Leicester Haymarket Theatre. Her film credits include: *Flickerman and the Ivory Skinned Woman* and *Psyche Out* (Pilgrim Films), *Season Ticket*, *Inbetween* and the BAFTA nominated *Bait* for Channel Four Films.

Malcolm Rippeth Lighting Designer

Malcolm has previously worked for Northern Stage lighting *The Selfish Giant*, *The Tiger's Bride* and *Pandora's Box*. Work elsewhere includes *Tear from a Glass Eye* at the Gate Theatre London, *Average White Girl* (Reconstructed) for the British Festival of Visual Theatre, *A Supercollider for The Family* and *Three Wishes* for Special Projects at Pleasance Edinburgh, *The Woolgatherer* at Battersea Arts Centre, *The Old Curiosity Shop* at Southwark Playhouse, and a revised version of *The Selfish Giant* for Leicester Haymarket. He has recently lit national tours of *Abyssinia* for Tiata Fahodzi and *A Billion Seconds* for Strathcona Theatre Company.

Richard Ryan Fight Director

Richard is Master-at-Arms at The Royal Academy of Dramatic Art. His numerous theatre credits include: *The Royal Family* (Haymarket Theatre); *The Three Musketeers* and *Romeo & Juliet* (Theatre Royal, York); *Clock Watching* (Stephen Joseph, Scarborough); *A Streetcar Named Desire* (Mercury Theatre, Colchester); *Bollocks* (RSC); *Dolly West's Kitchen* (National Theatre, Ireland/West End); *The Colleen Bawn* (Royal National Theatre); *The Duchess of Malfi* (Cheek by Jowl); *Macbeth* (Birmingham Rep.); *Liaisons Dangereuses* (Wolsey Theatre, Ipswich) and *Fantasy of a Kingdom* (Phuket Fantasea, Thailand) which featured a fight with 80 actors and four elephants.

Amanda Purvis Company Manager
Colin Holman Stage Manager
Nicola Irvine Deputy Stage Manager
Simon Henderson Assistant Stage Manager

Noir

Act One

Darkness. A lone voice sings 'Amazing Grace'. On the black screen the huge single word 'noir' appears in white. Other voices join in. A small, energetic man in a suit appears – the Evangelical Minister **Philip Lang**. *He stares at the audience, walks up and down as the hymn continues softly underneath. He speaks into a handheld microphone.*

Lang   I was lost, now I'm found. I was blind but now can see. (*Pause.*) I don't know if you read about this but last night a young woman's body was found in some woods. She'd been murdered. She was called Eve, this young girl and she was nineteen years old. (*Beat.*) How about that? Eve. Nineteen years old. (*Beat.*) God have mercy on her soul. (*Beat.*) There is a light, brothers and sisters, the light of truth, the light of love, the light of goodness and it's like . . . it's like electricity and it lights up this city. It's the light of thousands of souls. But when we lose the truth, when we lose the love, that light can grow dim. That light can go out. Then . . . then we are in darkness. (*Beat.*) I want to ask you a question . . . I want to ask you . . . are you found? Or are you still lost? Can you see? Or are you still blind? (*Beat.*) I want you to put your hands together and pray with me now . . .

The hymn ends abruptly and a spot snaps up on a Woman – **Ruth Hollis** *– handsome, smartly dressed, dark hair, standing at a lectern, her delivery a little automatic, the lecture one she has given many times before:*

Ruth   . . . But the character type perhaps most readily, though not necessarily accurately, identified with the genre is surely that of the private detective – variously referred to as the Shamus, the Snoop, Pinkerton or P.I. Two names are particularly revealing. Firstly the title 'private eye' – with its connotations of the excluded – the outsider – the voyeur – the detached observer of life. Secondly, and perhaps most relevantly . . . the Dick.

The spot snaps out on **Ruth** *as a heavy drum beat begins. At the same moment the words 'The Dick' appear on the black screen. A* **Waitress** *appears at the extreme stage right, holding a tray with two coffees and a sandwich on it. We are in a café. Two Customers sit in a booth seat, as yet unlit. A single light bulb is lowered from above, centre stage.*

Waitress   TWENTY-FOUR!

On the screen the words 'Four weeks Ago' appear.

Waitress   TWENTY-FOUR!

The beat cuts.

Ray   Could I have a light?

The lone bulb snaps on above the booth, revealing the two men: **George Hollis** *– forties, out of shape, nervous, respectable, and* **Ray Keyes** *– thirties, an intense air, odd.* **George** *is staring down at a photograph.* **Ray** *is leaning across the back of the booth, a cigarette in his mouth. The person in the seat behind him (all we can see is an arm) lights it for him.* **Ray** *exhales, the smoke curling up into the light above. Both men are wet and drunk. It's late at night. Outside it's raining.* **Ray** *wipes the water off his face.*

Ray (*to the person behind them*)   Ta. Fucking rain, eh?

The arm disappears again. **Ray** *sits back down and looks at* **George**.

Which former career? I've been lots of things, George. You see that?

He shoots a forearm out of his coat showing it to **George**.

See that? Seventh Armoured Brigade.

Waitress (*looking around*)   TWENTY-FOUR!

Ray   You ever hear about Al Jahra?

George   No. Who's that?

Ray   Place, George. Fuckin' place. Iraq. Al Jahra. You ever used a flamethrower?

George   No.

Ray   No.

The **Waitress** *has now disappeared into the opposite wings.*

Waitress (*offstage*)   TWENTY-FOUR!

Ray   Here!

The **Waitress** *stomps back on and, glaring at him, slops the coffees and sandwich on to the table. She crosses to the other side of the booth, talking to the unseen man under the following.*

George   Mickey . . . Mickey said you'd been in the police.

Ray (*eating*)   In the police?

George   Yes.

Ray   Yes. That is correct.

George   So, what happened?

Ray   I don't want to talk about that. That's . . . that's Chinatown.

George (*beat*)   Right. (*Pause.*) I'm such an idiot.

Ray   Well . . .

George   Where did they all go?

Ray   Some club.

George   I ruined the night.

Ray   It was a stag night, George. People get drunk. That's the point.

The **Waitress** *sits behind them, disappearing out of sight.*

George   I'm sorry about the sick.

Ray   It'll come out.

George   Such an idiot. Drank too much.

Ray   Well, you were upset . . . Drink your coffee.

George *sips his coffee.*

Ray   You feeling better?

George   Yeah. Thanks.

Ray   'S okay. (*Pause.*) So, you think your wife's fuckin' someone else?

George *stares at him.*

What? You brought it up.

George   I said . . . Never mind. I shouldn't have said anything.

Ray   Why not? We're friends aren't we?

George   Ray, I . . .

The **Waitress** *laughs suddenly on the other side of the booth.*

Ray (*pause*)   What?

George   Well, we don't really know each other, do we?

Ray   Well, exactly. Can't talk to close friends about this, can you? Fuckin' embarrassing. Why do you think she's fuckin' someone else?

George   Ray, I don't wanna talk about it.

Ray   Okay.

Pause. They drink their coffees.

George   She's dyed her hair blonde.

Ray (*beat*)   That's not exactly proof, George. 'Less she's dyed her muff.

George   What?

Ray   Has she dyed her muff?

George   What?

Ray   Nothing.

Pause. **George** *stares at the photograph.*

George   She killed Eric.

Ray   What?

George   My dog. She crashed the car. Eric went through the windscreen. She didn't care. I mean she didn't . . . she didn't even pretend to . . . I loved that dog. (*Beat.*) We . . . we used to have sex.

Ray   You and the dog?

George   Ruth and me. We used to . . . you know . . . it was regular. Now – nothing. She doesn't want me to touch her. (*Beat.*) I don't know . . . I don't know what women want. That's the truth. With Eric, you know, it was simple. You tickled his ears, he loved you.

Ray   Well, that's your basic difference between women and dogs. (*Beat.*) That her?

George *nods glumly.* **Ray** *takes the photograph and holds it up. A circle has been cut out of it.*

Ray   Where? That's half a head. Why's all this been cut out?

George   That's where my head was. (*Beat.*) She's started . . . she's started cutting my head out of the photographs. (*He's crying.*)

Ray   All right. All right. Come on.

George   I'm sorry.

Ray   'S all right.

George   This is . . . it was stupid. I . . . I married above myself.

Ray   Tall lass is she?

George   I'm a fuckin' idiot.

Ray   Hey – You haven't done anything wrong. You're not the one with someone else's cock in you, are you?

George *stands up.*

Ray   George . . .

George   I'm going home.

Ray (*standing*)   George, sit down. I'm just . . . I'm just paraphrasing, aren't I? Sit down.

George *sits down again.* **Ray** *sits.* **George** *wipes his eyes.*

Ray   Who do you think it is?

George (*beat*)   I don't know. Maybe . . . maybe somebody at work.

Ray   Where does . . . did you say Ruth?

George   Yeah.

Ray   Where does Ruth work?

George   The university. She's a lecturer. She thinks I'm a moron.

Ray   So maybe another lecturer? Maybe a student? Some fit teenager . . .

George *is crying again.*

Ray   Hey, you know, maybe no one at all. This stage you don't know anything, do you? (*Pause.*) You want me to find out?

George (*beat*)   What?

Ray (*patiently*)   Do you want me to find out if Ruth is having an affair?

George   No!

Ray   Yeah, right.

George   What?

Ray (*mimicking*)   'Mickey said you'd been in the police . . .'

George   What?

Ray   You know this is what I do.

George   No I don't! I thought you were a security guard at Fenwicks.

Ray   That's a – it's security operative – and that's a day job. I told you . . . I've done a lot of things. Do you want me to follow her? Yes or no?

George   No!

Ray   Okay.

Pause.

You sure?

George   Yes!

Ray   Okay. (*Beat.*) Up to you. (*Beat.*) You wanna stay in the dark.

The bulb above them flickers. We hear a loud crackling. **Ray** *stares up at it. It goes out – plunging us into darkness. Instantly we hear* **Howard Day** *singing a rendition of Abba's 'S.O.S.'. Slowly a light rises on* **Howard** *(in his forties).* **Howard** *wears smart middle-aged casual – exudes boy scout enthusiasm. He accompanies himself on a small keyboard. The lyrics to the song have been altered.*

Howard
    Where are those happy days?
    They seem so hard to find
    I try to reach for you
    But we have closed our minds
    We turned our backs on your love
    I wish I understood
    It used to be so nice
    It used to be so good
    So when you're near me
    Jesus can't you hear me?

S.O.S.
The love you gave us
Nothing else can save us
S.O.S.
When you're gone
Though I try, how can I carry on?

He finishes. Lights rise on **Lang**, *tie pulled loose, sitting in an easy chair, holding a cake. The words 'Two Weeks Ago' appear on the screen.* **Howard** *smiles at* **Lang** *expectantly.*

Lang   Well, now.

Howard   You see what I'm, I'm . . .

Lang   Oh, I think I do. I think that I do.

Howard   And that is just the beginning. We could take – you sure you're not too busy, Reverend Lang . . . ?

Lang *spreads his hands, smiling.*

Howard   We could take any song from the current pop charts and do the same thing. You know, there's some ministers, naming no names, I'm sure you know them, they're still, still talking about 'the devil's music'. Well, surprise, surprise – not too many young people in their congregations. What we're doing here is saying . . .

He produces a T-shirt emblazoned with the slogan 'Jesus – Top of the Pops!'

Jesus Sings Pop! Now, stop me if I'm, you know, but first of all, on behalf of the whole congregation, I wanted to say a big welcome . . .

He indicates the cake on **Lang**'s *lap.*

Lang   Thank you.

Howard   . . . and say how, how excited we all are that you should have come to us, because I think we can . . . we can really make a difference.

Lang (*smiling*)   Well, God bless you . . .

He puts the cake down and stands as **Howard** *continues.*

Howard   I've got so many ideas! Now, you take this . . .

He passes the T-shirt to **Lang** *and takes out a piece of paper.*

Howard (*putting on glasses*)   . . . Now, I've been looking into
some other titles, uh, Motown, Country, that sorta thing
and my daughter Alison, very talented young lady, she has
mentioned someone called the, the . . . (*He reads from the
sheet.*) . . . the Wutang Clan, which she thinks we can do
something with and that's very much what the young people
are listening to now.

Lang *smiles again*

Lang   Uhuh. Well, that's . . . that's . . . (*Beat.*) Now, these
T-shirts here, Mr Day, I think . . .

Howard   Howard.

Lang   . . . they're . . . Howard . . . I think they're just
terrific. Now, are these being sold?

Howard   Absolutely. Profits are going towards the
Pentecostal Community Project.

Lang   Isn't that something? I don't know where you find
the time. You work, don't you . . . .

Howard   Electrical goods.

Lang   And didn't you say something about the
Samaritans?

Howard   Well, I do a couple of shifts a week, yes. But you
know . . . when my wife died, I was very . . . I was very low
and . . . well, I like to be busy.

Lang   Righteous work, Mr Day. But you know, you can
do too much. (*Beat.*) Now, am I right in thinking you're also
currently secretary to the church?

Howard (*beat*)   Uhuh. That's . . . you sure I'm not
interrupting something here?

Lang   Not at all.

Howard (*beat*)   That's . . . currently secretary? Yes. (*Staring out the window.*) Look at . . . look at that view. You've got yourself a lovely view there.

Lang   Yes, yes I have. Reverend Wilson said that you had been very generous with your time in this respect?

Howard   Uhuh. I'm, uh . . . Reverend Wilson, God bless him, not a man for figures so I have been honoured to, uh, to help, help out in that capacity over the years. (*Of the view.*) See right down to the river.

Lang   So you have the accounts?

We begin to hear a low droning sound – almost a moan – building under the following lines. At the same moment an image fades up on the screen. It's a horserace in progress – the leaders racing in slow motion towards the finishing line.

Howard (*beat*)   The accounts?

Lang   You've kept the books?

Howard   Oh, yes. Uhuh. But I mean, I'm not an accountant, you understand . . .

Lang   No, that's all right. I am.

Howard (*beat*)   Is that . . . is that right?

Lang   By training, yes. Now, with the new charity status, I think it makes sense if I . . .

Howard   Yes! Makes sense. Right. You want to . . . you want to . . . ?

Lang   That's right. (*Of the T-shirt.*) These are really, very, very . . . (*He offers it back.*)

Howard   No. You keep that.

Lang   Oh, well . . . How much is that?

Howard   No, no . . .

Lang   Now, you said it was for charity didn't you?

Howard   Yes.

Lang   Then I think I should contribute, don't you? And about the books? Maybe you could bring them to the service tomorrow?

Howard *stands smiling and nodding vaguely. The drone builds and builds . . .*

Lang   How much is that? For the T-shirt?

The drone suddenly cuts. The horserace freezes on the screen.

Howard   Twenty thousand pounds.

Ruth *at her lectern. On the screen the words 'The Criminal' appear.*

Ruth   More than any other genre, film noir concerns itself with the morally ambiguous. The transgressor, the deviant, the criminal . . . is no longer simply the villain of the tale. He or she may indeed be the hero, enlisting the sympathies of the audience. In their revolt against society, against fate, against an absurd universe, the criminal becomes an existential . . .

She trails off, staring at someone in the audience. She holds her asthma inhaler.

Excuse me . . . could somebody . . . Excuse me . . .

She throws the inhaler at someone.

WAKE UP!

Ruth*'s office.* **Morris Talman** – *attractive, an aura of strange calm, holding a handkerchief to his eye – sits at her desk.* **Ruth** *joins him. On the screen the words 'Twelve Weeks Ago' appear.*

Ruth   I am so sorry.

Morris   No, it's . . .

Ruth   Is it okay? Let me see . . .

Morris   No, honestly, it's . . .

She examines his eye.

Ruth   I don't know what to say.

Morris   Really, it's fine. Would you like your inhaler back?

She takes it.

Ruth   Thank you. Listen, if you want to . . . I mean, there is a formal complaints procedure . . .

Morris   Oh, no that's . . .

Ruth   . . . and you have every right to . . .

Morris   . . . that's . . . I don't want to make a . . .

Ruth   I think you should. I really think you should make a complaint. I had no right.

Morris   It was . . . it was a really good shot.

Ruth (*beat*)   I don't . . . I don't know what got into me.

Morris   I just want to explain that . . .

Ruth   Well, you know, no . . . I mean, if you fall asleep that's . . . you have every right to fall asleep . . .

Morris   Yes, but . . .

Ruth   I mean, it happens all the time in lectures, and . . . I think that's why I, you know, it can be frustrating for, for . . .

Morris   Yeah, but the thing is . . .

Ruth   . . . but, you know, I really don't blame you. I mean, I bore myself with that lecture so . . . so, you know . . .

Morris   I wasn't asleep.

Ruth   Okay, well . . .

Morris   I really wasn't.

Ruth   Well, you had your eyes closed and . . .

Morris   I was listening. I was . . . I would never fall asleep in one of your lectures. Never.

Pause. Embarrassed, **Ruth** *flicks through some papers.*

Ruth   Well . . . that's . . . (*Beat.*) I'm sorry, I don't know your name . . . ?

Morris   Morris Talman.

Ruth   I've seen you in lectures, Morris, but I don't, uh, you're . . . are you post-grad?

Morris (*beat*)   No.

Ruth   Right. Whose tutorial group are you in?

Pause. She looks up from the papers.

Morris?

Morris   I don't know.

Ruth   You don't know?

Morris   I don't . . . I've never really gone to any tutorials.

Ruth (*beat*)   Morris, you don't go to tutorials you're not going to get your degree.

Morris   That's not important.

Ruth   That's not . . . ?

Morris   I couldn't get a degree..

Ruth (*beat*)   What do you mean?

Morris   I haven't enrolled.

Ruth   You haven't . . . you haven't . . .

Morris   No (*Beat.*) I didn't see why I should.

Ruth   You . . . you didn't see . . .

Morris   No. I'm sorry, but I don't think the qualification is the point. I considered it. I had an interview with this odd . . . a man with a hair lip?

Ruth   Professor Hughes?

Morris   Right. He was . . . he asked me if I was interested in the Badminton Club and . . . and I'm not. I'm not interested in that. And I'm not interested in the Chess Club or the Debating Society and I'm not really interested in qualifications. You know? I don't need that. I don't have the time. I'm interested in you.

Ruth (*beat*)   I'm sorry?

Morris   I read your book . . . *Images and Imagination?* That was a . . . that was a turning point for me. I only attend your lectures.

Pause. **Ruth** *pulls herself together.*

Ruth   Right. Well, you . . . you can't actually *do* that, Morris. You have to be enrolled to attend lectures.

Morris   If it's a question of money . . . ?

Ruth   It's not . . . well, there is that, but . . .

Morris   I have a ten-year plan. In ten years time there are certain films I want to be making. Until then I'm doing any work just to get by. At the moment I'm working as a waiter . . . so money is a little . . .

Ruth   That's not . . . How long have you been attending my lectures?

Morris   I'm in my third year now.

Ruth   Okay. Morris even if this was . . . which it definitely is *not* . . . the lectures alone can't . . . there is course work for example . . .

Morris   I've done all the course work. I mark them myself.

Ruth You mark your own essays?

Morris Yes. I think I've improved a lot this year. You think this is strange, don't you?

Ruth Yes, Morris. I think this is strange.

Morris 'All men who have turned out worth anything have had the chief hand in their education.' Walter Scott. (*Beat.*) I have never missed a single lecture. I have completed all of the course work. I have completed *all* of the optional work. I spend all day, every day, studying. There is a word for this . . .

Ruth Yes, there is . . .

Morris Passion.

Ruth That isn't the word I was thinking of . . .

Morris I'm *passionately* interested in film. I want to . . . I *need* to know more. Bertolucci, Fellini, Godard, Kieslowski, Kurosawa, Pasolini, Tarkovsky . . .

Ruth Was that alphabetical?

Morris Yes. (*Beat.*) I've written a film.

Beat. **Ruth** *sighs.*

Now just . . .

He takes out a manuscript and hands it to her.

Ruth Morris . . .

Morris I know . . .

Ruth I'm not a script editor, I'm not a . . .

Morris I know but . . . I think there's a chance I'm very talented. I know it seems unlikely but I think you should at least consider the possibility. Now this is a film, and you *know* film. If you think I'm wasting my time, just tell me and I will never bother you again. That's all.

Ruth looks at the title page.

Ruth   'Noir'.

Morris   It's a western.

Ruth *smiles.*

Ruth   Okay, look, I'll . . .

Morris   That's all I'm asking.

Ruth   But really . . .

Morris   I know. Absolutely. And I really appreciate this.

Pause. He takes out a silver cigarette case and holds it out to **Ruth**.

Ruth   I don't smoke.

Morris   I got it in an auction. It's the same case that Peggy Cummins used in *Gun Crazy*.

Ruth *takes the cigarette case.*

Morris   It's like the original Bonnie and Clyde . . . this couple go on a crime spree and . . .

Ruth   I know *Gun Crazy*.

Morris   Do you like it?

Ruth   Yes.

Morris   I knew you would.

She stares at the case in her hands.

Lights cut. We hear a **Man's** *voice speaking over a telephone line.*

Man   I want to die. (*Pause.*) Last night I walked all through Elswick. I was just hoping someone would try and mug me so I could resist and then they'd kill me. But . . . nothing. Even murderers ignore me. I just feel so, so, uh . . .

Lights snap up on **Howard** *in a small grey cubicle sitting listening to the* **Man** *on a phone.*

Howard   Lonely.

Man   So fucking lonely.

Howard Yes.

Man People find me strange. I think I depress people.

Howard (*depressed*) Uh-uh. (*Pause.*) Listen, Greg, would you . . .

Man Craig.

Howard . . . do some . . . sorry, Craig, would you do something for me?

Man What?

Howard I want you to quote the words of Mr David Bowie to yourself.

Man (*beat*) What?

Howard That's right. Mr Bowie, because . . . I know about loneliness. I lost my wife and I really . . . it's . . . (*Beat.*) When you're afraid to be alone, other people see it and don't like it. It scares them. So . . . what I want you to say to yourself, every day . . . are you listening, Craig?

Man Yes.

Howard Say to yourself . . . 'I'm not alone. (*Beat.*) No. No. I'm not alone.' Because you aren't alone, are you? Because someone is with you at all times in your life, aren't they?

Man (*beat*) What?

Howard That's right. God.(*Beat.*) That's right. So, you lose that fear. All right? That's your first step. Because once you've . . .

The Man hangs up. Pause. **Howard** *glances around him.*

That's right. Okay. God bless, then.

He hangs up. The phone rings again. Beat. **Howard** *picks up.*

Hello, Samaritans? (*Pause.*) Hello? Do you have a problem?

Alison's voice (*beat. Husky*) Yes.

Howard   Okay. Do you want to . . . do you want to tell me about it?

Alison   It's . . . I'm scared . . .

Howard (*pause*)   Uhuh. (*Beat.*) What are you scared of?

Alison   Someone's going to kill me.

Howard (*pause*)   You think . . . why do you think someone's going to kill you?

Alison   This man . . . my husband . . . he thinks . . . he thinks that I know something about him and I think he's going to kill me.

Howard   He . . . okay. He . . . what does he think you   ·
know?

Alison   I can't . . . I can't tell you that. I don't know . . . I don't know what I'm going to do . . .

Howard   Okay. Don't . . . uh . . . have you, have you gone to the police?

She hangs up. Pause. **Howard** *hangs up. Spotlight snaps up on* **Ruth** *at her lectern.*

Ruth   . . . as James Damico famously characterizes the situation: 'Either because he is fated to do so by chance, or because he has been hired for a job specifically associated with her, a man whose experience of life has left him sanguine and often bitter meets a not-innocent woman of similar outlook to whom he is sexually and fatally attracted . . .' This is the femme fatale.

On the screen the words 'The Femme Fatale' appear. Lights up on a telephone box with a young woman – **Alison Day** *– inside. The telephone box lends her, for a moment, a vague sense of captivity. She wears a fitted suit, black gloves, heels; her hair platinum blonde. She steps out of the box and begins to walk away.* **Morris** *appears behind her.*

Morris   Ruth?

Alison *walks on.*

Ruth!

Ray *appears between them, wearing a Micro-Scooter on his back. He stares after* **Ruth**. **Morris** *walks away.* **Ray** *produces a camera and quickly photographs* **Morris** *as he leaves. He photographs* **Alison** *as she disappears off-stage. He glances at his watch. The words 'Monday: Twelve fifteen' appear on the screen.*

Ray   Monday. Twelve fifteen. Contact.

On the screen a map of the city appears. A red line has been traced over certain streets.

Target comes out of university. Makes phone call. Approached by unknown man. They talk. Yak, yak. He heads back to the university. A student? Target heads . . .

He stops, considering, then stares up, looking hopefully for the sun. He takes out a cigarette.

(*Uncertainly.*) East? East. She crosses Percy Street, up St Mary's Place, round Sandyford, down Osborne Terrace, down Osborne Road, left on to Acorn Road . . .

He walks into an electrical goods store.

. . . takes a right up Georges Terrace and left into Sunbury Avenue.

He goes to light the cigarette he's still holding. **Howard** *in white shirt and tie walks past.*

Howard   I'm sorry, you can't smoke in here, sir.

Ray   Do you stock surveillance equipment?

Howard   No.

Ray   I'm looking for a Universal Infinity Bug, 'bout so big, looks like an ordinary phone socket . . .

Howard   You can't smoke in here, sir.

Ray   Right. Very good . . . (*He reads* **Howard**'s *name tag.*) Howard. You want to do your job? Go and check on the lad with the pink hair next to the Walkmans.

Howard   I'm sorry?

Ray   Young lad. Pink hair. Next aisle.

Howard   What about him?

Ray   Middle of winter he's walking round with his coat over one arm. Ring any alarm bells, Einstein? (*He lights the cigarette.*)

Howard (*beat*)   Sir, I'll have to call Security.

Ray   Let him finish his nap.

George *appears wearing suit and tie.*

George   It's all right, Harvey.

Howard   It's, uh, Howard.

George   Yes. Sorry. Howard.

Howard *leaves.*

Ray   Hello, George. I forgot you worked here.

George *smiles nervously.*

George   Hello, Ray. Are you okay?

Ray   I'm good, George.

George   What, what, what brings you here?

Ray   I'm interested in purchasing some bugging equipment, George.

George (*beat*)   We . . . we don't sell that sort of thing, Ray.

Ray   No?

George   No.

Ray   All right. I'll have a portable telly then.

George   Uhuh. Right. Well, we have a lot of different models. Why don't I get an assistant over? Could you . . . could you . . . ?

Ray   What?

George   Just . . . the cigarette?

Ray   Yeah. No problem.

He continues to smoke. **George** *stands uncertainly.*

George   Right. I'll, I'll go and . . . (*He turns and begins to walk away.*)

Ray   I saw your wife yesterday.

Pause. **George** *comes back.*

George   I'm sorry?

Ray   Your wife, Ruth. I think I saw her yesterday. In Jesmond. Think it was her. From the photo I mean. Nice looking. Blonde hair. Suit. Younger than you, yeah?

George   A bit. (*Beat.*) She was teaching yesterday.

Ray   Right. Must have been mistaken.

George *stares at him, then turns and walks away. He comes back.*

George   Where was she?

Ray   Fifty-nine, Sunbury Avenue.

George   You . . . you followed her?

Ray   No, just saw her in the street.

George   I told you no!

Ray   Just coincidence, George.

George (*pause*)   In a house.

Ray   Big house.

George   Supposed to be teaching. What was she doing in a house in Jesmond?

Ray   Well, I got round the back, up on the wall and had a look through the window . . .

George   You what?

Ray   You wanna know or not?

George (*pause*)   Know what?

Ray   Big room, woman sitting down, talking to your wife.

George   A woman?

Ray   Woman. Your wife takes her coat off . . .

George   Uhuh . . .

Ray   Stands on a table.

George   Uhuh . . .

Ray (*beat*)   That's it.

George (*beat*)   That's . . . that's . . . What d'ya mean?

Ray   She just stood on the table. 'Bout ten minutes.

George   On a table?

Ray   Yep. Talking. On a table.

George   What the fuck . . . Did it . . . Did it look like . . . ?

Ray (*beat*)   What?

George (*beat*)   You think it was a . . . a lesbian thing?

Ray   I don't know. Is your wife a lesbian?

Pause. **George** *considers.*

George   How would you know? (*Beat.*) On a table? (*Beat.*) What do you think it means?

Ray   Your wife got any history of narcotics?

George   What?

Ray   She a user?

George   Ruth?

Ray   You never know, George. Not even with your nearest and dearest. Take Mickey for example?

George   Mickey? Mickey does drugs?

Ray   We're not here to talk about Mickey.

George (*beat*)   So what happened after that?

Ray   I dunno. I had to get back to work.

George   Fuckin' hell, Ray! Couldn't you have taken a sicky?

Ray (*coldly*)   I don't know, George. Does the shoplifter take a sicky? (*Beat.*) Do you recognize this man?

He shows **George** *a photograph. The photograph – of* **Morris Talman** *with his back to us – appears on the screen.*

George   What? I . . . I don't know. I can't see his face. Couldn't you get his face?

Ray   Yeah, I would have done, only I thought that might have the given the game away just a tiny bit.

George   Who is he?

Ray   'S what I'm asking.

George (*beat*)   What was she doing on a table? In Jesmond?

Ray   'S what we're gonna find out.

George (*pause*)   I don't . . . no. No.

Ray   No, what?

George   You can't keep . . . It's . . . it's not right.

Ray *stares at him. Pause.*

George   What if she realized she was being followed?

Ray   I'm The Shadow, George.

A Chinese restaurant. **Morris**, *in a waiter's coat, approaches* **Ray**.

Ray (*to the waiter*)   Table for one.

The word 'Tuesday' appears on the screen.

Tuesday. Lunch break. Ring the university. Ruth Hollis isn't in her office. On a hunch I bicycle it down to Sunbury Avenue and sure enough as I'm coming down the road she's coming up. I ride straight past. I let her get a good block away before I turn. She's down Georges Terrace and I'm after her, always one block back, or riding parallel to her down Grosvenor Place. She's back at Percy Street but she goes past the university, right up St Andrews and left on to Stowell Street. 'Bout halfway up she goes into a door next to a restaurant. I padlock the bike up. Door's got one of those little plaques next to it. Says Telco. Next thing I'm in the restaurant across the road, corner table, keeping an eye out, I'm blending and no – she doesn't know she's being followed.

Ray *sits at a table as* **Alison** *arrives next to him.*

Alison   I think I'm being followed.

Ray *stares at her. She sits beside him.*

Please, just . . . just talk to me like we know each other.

Ray   Uh . . .

Alison   Can you see the man over my shoulder?

Ray   Which one?

Alison   There's only one.

Ray   Yes.

Alison   He's been following me.

Ray (*beat*)   Right. Is he . . . Is that . . . Do you want me to . . . you sure, are you?

Alison   I think so. Is he still there? Don't look!

Ray I can't see, without looking.

Alison Say something and I'll laugh . . . like we're relatives or something.

Ray *stares at her, thinking.*

Ray Your Uncle John's died.

Alison (*beat*) What?

Ray (*beat*) Your Uncle John's died?

Alison What are you talking about?

Ray Nothing. What?

Alison What are you talking about?

Ray Nothing, I'm just . . . you know, just first thing came into me head.

Alison How did you know about Uncle John?

Ray (*beat*) What?

Alison How did you know I had an Uncle John?

Ray I . . . I didn't. I just made it up. Just for something to say.

Alison That's not funny. I've got an Uncle John. Jesus.

Ray I didn't know. It just sounded like a family thing. Sorry.

Alison (*beat*) That was weird. Fancy saying that and . . . God. Wasn't that weird? Is he still there?

Ray *glances surreptitiously over his menu.*

Ray He's going.

Alison Thank God. I'm really sorry about this.

Ray That's all right. Do you want me go and have a word with him?

Alison No!

Ray   Okay. (*Beat.*) Why's he following you?

Alison (*beat*)   I can't tell you that.

They stare at each other. **Morris** *approaches.*

Morris   Are you ready to order?

Alison   Oh, I'm not . . . (*To* **Ray**.) I'm sorry, I'm interrupting your . . . I'll go.

Ray   You don't have to go. I mean . . .

Alison   Really?

Ray   Yeah, I mean if you're gonna eat anyway . . .

Alison   I was gonna eat . . . I mean I'm on my lunch.

Ray   Well, you know . . . It's Chinese here.

Alison   I know. This is Chinatown.

Ray   I know.

Morris (*beat. Sighing*)   I'll give you a bit longer.

He walks off. **Ray** *stares after him.*

Ray   I know him from somewhere.

Alison   What?

Ray   Waiter. Did you notice he wasn't Chinese? (*Beat.*) That's quite unusual.

Alison   I still can't get over you saying Uncle John. You know what would be really weird?

Ray   What?

Alison   If Uncle John did die today.

Ray   Yeah. That would . . . that would be weird.

Pause.

Alison   He died two years ago.

Ray   Right. I'm sorry.

Alison   Yeah. Kidneys. What's your name?

Ray (*beat*)   Dave. David. Hello. Hockney.

Alison   Really?

Ray (*beat*)   Yes.

Alison   Like the painter?

Ray (*beat*)   Yes.

Alison *stoops to her bag to get cigarettes. As she does so,* **Ray** *punches himself in the head. She sits up again.*

Alison   God. That must be really strange.

Ray   Huh. What's yours?

Alison   Have a guess. See if you can do it again.

Ray *stares at her. She goes to light her cigarette. Pause.*

Ray   Ruth.

She freezes with the cigarette in her mouth.

Alison (*beat*)   Oh my God.

We hear the furious buzz of a power drill. Lights rise on **Ruth** *sitting next to her psychiatrist,* **Dr Meyers** *– crumpled and irritable, staring at some papers on her lap. On the screen we see the words 'Ten Weeks Ago'. Both women sit for a moment, enduring the noise. Finally the drill stops.*

Dr Meyer (*bored*)   Where do you think this anger is coming from?

Ruth   I don't know. I . . . it's everything. The students. I have a second-year student thought Fellini was a make of tyre. Why . . . you care that little about film, why would you choose the course? I hate my job. Hate the students, hate the staff . . .

Dr Meyer   Uhuh. How are things at home?

Ruth   Home? Oh, home's great. I was watching him eat last night, and he makes this, this chomping noise, makes me wanna stab him and I'm thinking, you could leave him . . .

Dr Meyer   Well, you could leave him . . .

Ruth   No, I can't leave him, because he's like this big, stupid dog and if you leave him it's like leaving a big, stupid dog on the motorway. I'm just . . . I feel paralysed. There's nothing I can do. I just have to wait for one of us to die. And that could take years. (*Beat.*) There's a student at . . . well, actually he isn't but . . . I don't know if he's interesting or . . . retarded. I don't understand men. (*Beat.*) I could have an affair.

Dr Meyer   You could have an affair . . .

Ruth   Are you . . . are you doing a crossword?

We hear the sound of hammering. **Ruth** *closes her eyes in irritation.*

This . . . this noise . . .

Dr Meyer   I'm sorry?

Ruth (*louder*)   Do we have to have this noise?

Dr Meyer   Oh God, don't get me started. I have this all day. New conservatory. How a conservatory can take this long I do not know.

The hammering stops.

They are driving me fucking crazy. (*Beat.*) So . . . your husband . . .

Ruth   No, it's . . . it's not him. It's me. When my mother died . . . I was pretty young . . . we all gathered around the bed in the hospital and – I've got three sisters – we were saying our goodbyes, you know, one by one. And when it got to my turn she suddenly looked at me and she . . . she looked furious . . . I mean, you've never seen anyone look so . . . it was like she wanted to hit me. So for, for years I had this, this guilt thing, because it was like she knew I'd done something really terrible, but I didn't know what. (*Beat.*) But, I mean, the funny thing is . . . I have never done a single wrong thing in my life. Not really. Nothing. And just recently I started to think, what if that's why she was angry? Maybe she was pissed off because she knew I was going to become the most boring fucker in the world.

Dr Meyer (*beat*)   Uhuh. (*To herself, re. crossword.*) Amazonian!

Ruth   What?

Dr Meyer   If you could talk to your mother now, what do you think you would say?

Ruth *considers. We hear the opening chords to 'I Want You Back' by the Jackson Five. Lights cut and rise on the electrical goods store.* **Howard** *in his shirt and tie is demonstrating a keyboard to a* **Customer**. *He sings as he plays the opening verse.*

The **Customer** *is staring at him.* **Howard** *stops.*

Howard (*beat*)   I'm adapting it.

Customer   So has this got any drums or anything on it?

Howard   Oh, it's got everything. There's twenty-seven backing tracks – you just change the chord with your left hand. Would you like to try?

Customer   Well . . . I'm not very musical.

He joins **Howard** *at the keyboard.*

Howard   Honestly, you don't need to be. These days they play themselves. You can scroll through the different voices here . . .

The Customer glances around them.

Customer   So . . .

He glances at the name tag **Howard**'s *wearing.*

. . . it's Howard isn't it?

Howard   That's right.

Customer   So . . .

He head-butts **Howard** *savagely.* **Howard** *stumbles back clutching his face.*

So pay your fucking debts, Howard.

He moves to walk away then comes back. He plays a bar of 'Chopsticks', then leaves. **Howard** *holds his face, checking to see if anyone is watching. A clash of Chinese cymbals. Lights up on the Chinese restaurant.* **Ruth** *and* **Morris** *sit at a table.* **Ruth** *has her eyes closed.*

Ruth   'But I'm scared. For the first time, I'm really scared, because I'm happy and I love you, and it's too big. It's . . . I want to hide it under a stone, I want to hide this happiness in case people see it, but it's too big, it's like a *Cathedral* and . . . I love you.'

She glances at the script on the table in front of her.

And then he says . . .

Morris (*smiling*)   'Eat your eggs.'

Ruth   Yes, which is from . . .

Morris   *Sullivan's Travels.*

Ruth   Yes! Which is so perfect! And it just . . . it ties together that whole journey! It's . . . it's . . .

Morris   You like it?

Ruth   I . . . I do. (*Pause.*) Sometimes students give me scripts but they're . . . you know . . . I get a lot of brains exploding, Necrophilic Rom-Coms . . . that kind of thing. I just . . . I wasn't expecting this. Can I ask you something? When she steals the book, near the beginning . . . what was the idea behind that?

Morris   I think . . . I think I meant 'The distance is nothing. It's only the first step that is difficult.'

Ruth stares at him for a moment. She rouses herself.

Ruth   Yes . . . and, and the Waitress is such a beautiful character. So . . . is she . . . I mean, is it autobiographical?

Morris   Up to a point. I mean, a lot had to change. She's a woman. And I'm not.

Ruth   No.

Morris   So, you know . . . imagination. I think it needs more work.

Ruth   Well, I don't know. I wouldn't know what to . . . it's . . . it's beautiful, Morris.

Morris   You know what I'd like? I'd like us to work on it together. I really think you could help me lift this up to another level.

Ruth   Oh, that's . . . but, you know . . . I'm not a writer.

Morris   You don't know what you are yet.

Pause.

Ruth   Can I ask . . . what are you planning to do with the script?

Morris   Well, there's some contacts I'd like to chase up from when I was in the industry.

Ruth   You've worked in the film industry?

Morris   In a small way.

Ruth   Shorts?

Morris   Porn.

Ruth (*beat*)   Right . . . you . . . you made porn films?

Morris   I directed them for a while. I starred in some as well. I have an unusually large penis, so . . . (*Beat.*) I'm sorry, is this embarrassing you?

Ruth   No, not . . . not . . . not at all.

She stares intently at the menu.

I was thinking about having the Egg Fu-Yung

Morris   I wouldn't. Chef's in one of his moods.

Ruth   Right. (*Beat.*) So . . . you . . . you don't do *that* any more?

Morris   No. I got restless. In the end I felt narrative was so much more erotic than just filming sex. I was working on this one . . . 'Anal Alien Onslaught' and I started to add a lot of plot, just, you know, constantly re-working it, and then they realised there weren't any aliens in it any more. Or anal sex. So I got fired. Can I ask you something?

Ruth   Yes?

Morris   Have you tried meditation before? You seem very tense all the time.

Ruth   Uh, no. No, I haven't.

Morris   Just an idea. It really helped me find focus in my life.

He stands up and takes out a pad.

I should take your order.

Ruth   Right. (*Beat.*) I haven't had sex for three years.

Morris (*beat*)   Right.

Pause. She studies the menu, fiercely embarrassed.

Ruth   I'll have the Szechuan Beef.

Morris notes it down and leaves. Ruth stares ahead. Lights rise on a toilet in a department store. **Ray** *stands smoking, in his mac.*

Ray   Not at all the way you'd think she'd be. You know – university type . . . you think bit stuck up, bit of a cunt, but she was . . . she was very . . .

He pauses, thinking about her. He takes off his mac, revealing his security guard uniform underneath.

Question is, who's the bloke following her? Apart from me, I mean. (*Beat.*) Anyway, I rang George and told him that the surveillance was going well and this time I'd stuck to her all afternoon. (*Beat.*) I missed out the bit about having lunch with her. (*Beat.*) And then some drinks.

Morris Talman *arrives at the toilet and begins to quickly bundle some items of clothing into a sports bag.* **Ray** *produces his cap and puts it on. On the screen the words 'Two Weeks ago' appear.* **Ray** *bangs on the imaginary cubicle wall.*

Ray   Could you come out of the cubicle, sir?

Morris (*bundling clothing*)   Sorry?

Ray   Come out, please.

Morris   I won't be a minute.

Ray   Come out now, please.

Morris *finishes and 'steps out' of the cubicle.*

Morris   What?

Ray   What's in your bag, sir?

Morris   In the . . . ? Nothing. It's just my sport's kit.

Ray   Can I look in the bag, sir?

Morris   No. No, I don't think so.

Ray (*beat*)   All right, listen. If you . . . what's your name?

Morris   Morris.

Ray   If you go outside, Morris . . . they'll nick you. All right? They'll nick you. You'll get a fine, you got previous, you could go down.

Morris   Look, there's nothing in the . . . the bloody bag!

Ray   I'm asking – watch the language, all right? – I'm asking you to show me what's in your bag so we can stop it now, right? I don't want to see you going to prison, ruining your life, for what? For a few quids' worth of T-shirts?

Morris   I haven't got any T-shirts!

Ray   Or whatever . . .

Morris   I haven't got any bloody . . .

Ray   Whatever. That was an example. And WATCH
THE LANGUAGE. Now . . . give me the bag.

Morris   I'm sorry, no.

Ray   Give me the . . .

Morris   No!

Ray *reaches for the bag.* **Morris** *goes to shove him, but* **Ray** *spins
him round, grabs his hair and plunges him head first down into the
toilet bowl.*

Ray   NOW I WAS NICE, WASN'T I? I WAS
FUCKING POLITE WITH YOU, WASN'T I?

He drags **Morris***'s head, minus glasses, out of the toilet, dripping
wet. He gasps for air.*

WASN'T I FUCKIN' POLITE WITH YOU?

Morris (*gasping*)   You . . .

Ray *pushes him back into the bowl.*

Ray   LITTLE BIT OF FUCKING BASIC DECENCY!

*He drags him out again, slams the toilet lid down and bangs the head
he's holding off it several times. Finally he lets him go and stands up.*
Morris *lies gasping for breath.* **Ray** *picks up his bag and unzips it.*

Morris   It's just me sports kit!

Ray *pulls out a long black silk dress.*

Ray   I see you're a keen golfer.

Morris (*pause*)   All right, this is . . . you can't . . . there was
no need for this kind of hostility. I'm going to have to see
someone.

Ray   That right?

Morris   Yes, that's right!

Ray *draws a black Y-shaped object from his trouser belt. Despite himself,* **Morris** *flinches.*

Ray (*beat*)   You seen one of these before? (*Pause.*) No, I bet you haven't. (*Pause.*) 1933. Victor Appleton writes *Tom Swift in the Land of Wonders* – one in a series of children's books featuring the young adventurer and inventor – Tom Swift. In this particular novel Tom invents a special weapon, known as the electrical rifle.

Ray *holds up the object.*

Thomas A. Swift's Electrical Rifle. (*Beat.*) Taser. (*Beat.*) Fifty thousand volts, puts you down, you get up quiet. Originally described as a non-lethal weapon. Now described as a less-lethal weapon on account of several people dying and if I hear one more word from you I will electrocute your cock up until the point where it drops off onto the floor.

Pause. **Ray** *picks up the dress from where it fell on the floor and throws it over his shoulder.*

Morris   Look, I'm sorry. It was . . . it's a friend of mine . . . a girlfriend . . . it's her birthday . . .

Ray   Buy her a decent boyfriend.

He throws the empty bag at him.

Morris   Could I have my glasses back?

Ray *fishes the glasses out of the toilet and throws them at* **Morris**.

Ray   Go on. Drift.

Morris *grabs his bag and hurries away.*

(*After him.*)

And tell your friends: Do Not Fuck With Fenwicks.

Ray *examines the dress, then bundles it inside his jacket. Lights rise on* **Ruth** *at her lectern.*

Ruth   . . . while Borde and Chaumeton also noted as characteristic of the genre the use of both 'flashback' and 'voice-over narrative'. It could be argued that both serve to further unsettle the viewer: flashback removing the illusion of narrative freedom – we are 'doomed' to observe what has already happened and cannot be changed; whilst 'voice-over narrative' robs us of any security we might have found in an omnipotent narrator. The story is being told to us from one person's viewpoint only. We may not find their version of events entirely accurate.

Howard's *voice is heard over the speakers.*

Howard's voice   I suppose you'll call this a confession when you hear it. I just . . . I just wanted you to understand how this all, all got started. I remember it really clearly. It was the first time for me and uh . . . yep. That was it. (*Beat.*)

Howard *is revealed sitting miserably at a desk.*

This was about two years ago . . .

On the screen the words 'FLASHBACK' *flash on and off. A female* **Doctor** *walks across stage, holding something.*

I wasn't very happy at the time. Helen was dead. I don't know . . . my faith was pretty low and I was having . . . problems.

The **Doctor** *sits behind her desk and pulls a flip chart towards her. She flips the first page, revealing a large cross-section diagram of a penis. The music cuts.* **Howard** *stares at the diagram. Pause.*

Doctor   Don't worry. It's not to scale.

She laughs a little. **Howard** *stares at the diagram.*

Doctor   Okay. The implant would be inserted here . . . very small scar . . . very straightforward procedure . . .

She begins to rhythmically squeeze the small inflation bladder in her hand.

... then to gain the, uh, the erection you would simply
inflate like this. Takes a . . . takes a minute or so. And to, ah,
to deflate there is this valve here. Not, not hard at all. (*Beat.*)
Difficult. At all.

*She shows him the device. Pause. From somewhere offstage comes the
faint sound of a radio horserace commentary.*

Howard's voice   And from somewhere else I could just
hear this horserace on the radio. I could hear all the names.

On the screen we see the horses racing once more in slow motion.

Doctor   Is your wife being . . . understanding?

Howard (*beat*)   She's dead.

Doctor   Oh . . .

Howard   This is . . . this is just for me.

Doctor (*beat*)   Uhuh. (*Beat.*) Well, as I said this is . . . this is
the final option. And the chances are the answer is much,
much simpler.

Howard (*beat*)   Yellow King.

The image on screen freezes.

Doctor   Sorry?

Howard   Sorry. Just the . . . the horserace there.

Doctor   Oh. Yes. You a gambling man?

Howard   No. I never gamble.

Doctor   It's the electrician. I'll tell him to turn it down.

She walks out. **Howard** *stands and stares up at the frozen image of
running horses.*

Howard's voice   It was like I saw the name written in
my head. And on the way out I asked the electrician who'd
won. And he said Yellow King. And right then and there I
started to feel myself again.

Howard *puts his hands in his pockets. A beat begins.*

Not long after, I went in to a Casino for the first time. I just remember the noise . . . all those . . . all those wheels moving. And music. They were always playing music. I think the first thing I heard was 'Down Town'. It was just like home.

A hotel casino – early evening. **Howard** *stands staring at a* **Gambler** *placing bets on the roulette table. A bored woman* **Croupier** *stands behind. She spins the wheel. In the background we hear a muzak version of 'Down Town'.*

Croupier No more bets. (*Pause.*) Thirty-two rouge.

She sweeps the chips from the table.

Place your bets.

The **Gambler** *turns away and sips his drink.*

Gambler   Got to know when to hold 'em, when to fold 'em . . . .

Howard *smiles.*

Howard   Kenny Rogers. (*Pause.*) It's very quiet isn't it?

Gambler   Early days.

Croupier (*to* **Howard**)   Betting, sir?

Howard   Oh, no . . . thanks. I don't . . . don't gamble.

Gambler   Lost, are you?

Howard   Ha! Yes . . . I know. (*Beat.*) I'm handing out some leaflets.

Gambler   Yeah. What leaflets?

Howard   Samaritans.

Gambler   Give me one. I'll need that later.

He takes a leaflet from **Howard**. *Pause.*

Howard (*to the* **Croupier**)   It looks very complicated.

The **Croupier** *smiles politely.*

Howard   Is it?

Croupier   What's that, sir?

Howard   Is it complicated?

Croupier (*bored*)   Numbers thirty-five to one, splits seventeen to one, corners eight to one, six line five to one, street eleven to one, dozens two to one, outside bets one to one.

Howard (*pause*)   Right.

Gambler   So, how come you don't gamble?

Howard   Oh, I just . . . I don't . . . I don't think I would like it.

Gambler   Don't know 'til you try.

Howard   I don't think I would.

Gambler   Bet you ten pound you would.

Howard *smiles. The* **Gambler** *picks up a chip and hands it to him.*

Gambler   Have a go on me.

Howard   Oh, no, I don't think . . .

Gambler   Go on. I'm only gonna lose it anyway.

Howard   No, honestly. I don't know what to do.

Gambler   There's nothing to know. 'S just chance. Pick a number.

Howard *hesitates, then places the chip on a number. The* **Croupier** *sighs and spins the wheel.*

Croupier   Place your bets.

Howard *watches the wheel spin.*

Howard   I . . . uh . . . I read this thing said that uh, 'Accident manifests the will of God.'

The **Gambler** *stares at him blankly.*

Gambler   That right?

Howard *nods, staring at the wheel.*

Croupier   No more bets.

Lights cut. Rise on a park. Afternoon. **Ray** *stands facing the audience. He wears a Hawaiian shirt and pants. He's holding half a loaf of sliced bread. He takes a slice out, tears a piece off and throws it out into the audience. Pause.*

Ray (*to ducks*)   What's the matter? (*Beat.*) What's the matter with it? (*Beat.*) Here.

He eats some.

Umm. Good. See, it's . . .

He spits the bread out.

That's . . . that's just a bit of mould. That's okay. Here . . .

He throws another piece. Beat.

It's white bread. It's . . . you don't like white bread?

He throws a larger piece.

You . . . It's what you eat! You wanna stay that size all your life? (*Beat.*) What are you staring at it for? It's just white bread!

He hurls the rest of the loaf. Beat.

Fuckin' ducks.

Ray *sits at a a park bench and stares out. He lights a cigarette.* **Alison** *appears, wearing a coat.* **Ray** *stares at her intently.*

Ray   You're late. (*Beat.*) Are you wearing it?

She opens the coat to reveal the dress **Morris** *had stolen.*

Ray   It looks . . . you look . . .

He holds his hands up in a vague gesture.

Alison   I can't keep the dress, Dave.

Ray (*beat*)   Right. Well, you know . . . I don't know anything about clothes. It's uh . . . give's it back and I'll get you something else. I'll get you a toaster.

Alison   I can't see you any more, Dave.

Ray *stares out at the lake, smoking.*

Pause.

Ray (*beat*)   You see those ducks? Can hardly move on that lake for fuckin' bread. Life's so fuckin' easy for them they want . . . they want fuckin' . . . croissants or something. You think those ducks are happy? You seen their eyes? Blank. Totally blank. They're like . . . they're like the Stepford Ducks. Life's too safe for them. What I should do is come back here with a fuckin' rifle, you know? SKS carbine. Sounds cruel . . . but I'm telling you . . . the next morning, the survivors would wake up glad to be alive.

Alison (*pause*)   Aren't you cold?

Ray   You spend enough time fighting in the desert, you don't mind the cold. (*Beat.*) Why can't you see me any more?

Alison   I don't want you getting hurt.

Ray   I won't get hurt. I love you.

Alison   What are you . . . we've only had dinner a few times, Dave. You don't know me.

Ray   I know you. I think about you all the time. I can't stop . . .

Alison   All right, listen to me. There's things I haven't told you. (*Beat.*) There was another man. Before you.

Ray   That's . . . that doesn't matter. It's us that matters now.

Alison   He's . . . he's dangerous, Dave.

Ray   You don't have to worry about . . .

Alison   No, listen to me! He's really dangerous. He's mixed up in some . . . I don't know . . . he knows some bad people.

Ray   What do you mean? (*Beat.*) Drugs?

Alison   Yes. Yes, I think so.

Ray   That doesn't scare me, Ruth.

Alison   That's not it. (*Beat.*) I found . . . I found a picture.

Ray (*beat*)   What kind of picture?

Alison   It was in his desk. A Polaroid . . .

Ray   Ruth . . . what kind of picture?

A black-and-white, grainy photograph fades in on the screen . . . a woman lying face=down in woods.

Alison   A dead woman. (*Beat.*) It was a picture of a dead woman . . . in some woods. I found it in his desk. (*Beat.*) I think he murdered her. He came in when I was closing the drawer. Next time I looked, it was gone. Since then, I've got the feeling he's been having me watched. Like the day we met. I think he wants to see if I know . . . I think he's gonna kill me, Dave.

Ray (*beat*)   Who is he?

Alison   What? You don't know . . .

Ray grabs her arms.

Ray   Who is he?

Alison   It doesn't matter who he . . .

Ray   WHO IS HE?

Alison (*frightened*)   He's called . . . he's called Lang! He's called Philip Lang!

She pulls herself loose.

Ray   All right. Listen to me. I'm going to take care of this for you.

Alison   What?

Ray   What did you think? Did you think I would just leave you?

He pulls his shirt open. RUTH is tattooed in huge letters across his chest.

You're on my heart, Ruth. You're on my heart.

Alison   Oh, Jesus . . .

She runs off.

Ray (*shouting after her*)   Ruth! RUTH!

He stares out at the lake.

What are you looking at? (*Beat.*) What are you looking at?

Lights cut and rise on **Howard** *sitting in a chair, trying to look relaxed.* **Lang** *stands beside him, filing his nails. On the screen the words 'Last Week' appear.*

Howard   . . . Yes, now . . . yes, I can explain that. That's the . . . (*Beat.*) Yes. That money's in a separate account. I set up a separate account, high interest, for the grant money we received for the community projects I mentioned and I moved some money over there, for the, for the fiscal year.

Lang   For the fiscal year.

Howard   That's right.

Lang (*beat*)   Good. That's that, then.

Howard   I can move that back over, but I think there's a penalty for withdrawal before a certain period so maybe we should wait until, until . . .

Lang   Absolutely.

Howard   Yes?

Lang   Absolutely.

Howard   Okay. (*Beat.*) Okay, then.

Lang *laughs good-naturedly.* **Howard** *smiles uncertainly.*

Lang   Your face . . .

Howard   My . . . ?

Lang   God love you, you'd think I was accusing you of something!

Howard *laughs.*

Howard   No, I . . . I knew you just meant . . .

Lang *smiles.*

Lang   Yes, well, I am accusing you of something, you piece of shit.

Howard's *laugh trails away. Pause.*

Howard   I'm sorry?

Lang   I said I am accusing you of something, you thieving piece of shit.

Howard (*beat*)   I don't . . . I don't . . .

Lang   Get on your knees.

Howard   . . . I don't know . . . what?

Lang   GET ON YOUR KNEES!

Howard *gets on his knees.* **Lang** *places his hand on* **Howard**'s *forehead.*

Do you believe in the death and resurrection of our Lord Jesus Christ?

Howard   Yes.

Lang   Do you believe in the unity of believers in the Body of Christ?

Howard   Yes.

Lang Do you believe Jesus made a full, perfect and sufficient sacrifice for the sins of mankind?

Howard Yes.

Lang Where's the money?

Howard I . . .

Lang Where's the money?

Howard I borrowed it.

Lang Where's the money?

Howard I . . .

Lang Where's the money?

Howard (*beat*) I stole it. (*Beat.*) I owed some people money because . . . I've been gambling. I'm a gambler. I want to stop but I owed . . . I didn't know what else to do and . . . (*Beat.*) I stole it.

Pause.

Lang We have been . . . we have been spreading here, Howard. We have been spreading light here. The UK Evangelical Alliance has been spreading light. The International Communion of Charismatic Churches has been spreading light. The Global Gospel Fellowship has been spreading light. Our website and our newspaper and all our projects . . . they've been spreading light. But shit like you . . . you destroy the light, Howard.

Howard No one has to . . .

Lang What?

Howard No one has to . . .

Lang I can't hear you Howard. I can't hear you!

Howard No one has to know. I can get the money back. I can give you it back. No one will ever know. I just . . . I need a little time.

Lang (*pause*)   You have one week. One week, then I call the police.

Alison *walks in. Pause.* **Howard** *smiles at her anxiously.*

Howard   Reverend Lang, this is . . . this is my daughter Alison.

Lang (*smiling*)   Call me Philip, Alison. How are you?

Alison (*beat*)   I'm good.

Lights snap out and rise on **Ray** *sitting in a chair facing us. A beat begins to softly build underneath. On the screen the word 'Today' appears.*

Ray (*softly*)   Put it down. (*Beat.*) Put it down, Lang. (*Beat.*) That's better. (*Beat.*) I know about you, Lang. I know about the photograph. I know about the girl. Don't you move! You're coming with me, Lang. Yes, you are. (*Beat.*) Well then, maybe you'd like to meet my friend here.

He draws the Taser.

Nineteen thirty-three. Victor Appleton writes *Tom Swift in the Land of Wonders* – one in a series of children's books . . .

A **Barber** *approaches.* **Ray** *quickly hides the Taser.*

Barber   Sorry about that, sir.

He drapes a barber's apron around Ray.

What can I do for you?

Ray   Shave it off. (*Beat.*) Shave it all off.

The **Barber** *produces a pair of scissors. We cut to black as music erupts.*

Act Two

Darkness. The heavy beat begins. On the screen the huge single word 'noir' begins to cross-fade into the photograph of the girl in the woods. A large moon begins to glow. The beat settles into a low heartbeat. A torchlight flashes across the stage. Woods. Night. **Howard** *crosses, picking his way carefully through the undergrowth, by the light of a torch he's holding. He is leading his daughter* **Alison**. *Both wear coats. A black hood covers* **Alison**'s *head.* **Howard** *stops and stares around him. He glances at his watch. Pause.*

Alison   Dad?

Howard   Yes, love?

Alison   I don't want my surprise any more.

Howard *sighs.*

Howard   Now . . . what did I say?

Alison   I know . . . it's just . . . I don't like woods. It's cold . . .

Howard   Well, didn't I say wear the jumper?

Pause.

Alison   Where's mam?

Howard (*beat*)   Are you having a nice time?

Alison (*without enthusiasm*)   Uhuh.

Howard *glances at his watch.*

Alison   Is mam meeting us here?

Howard (*still staring at the watch*)   Here we go . . . five, four, three, two . . . Happy Birthday!

Alison   Thanks. (*Beat.*) Where's the surprise?

Howard   Hang on. Something missing here.

He takes a paper party hat out of his pocket and puts it on top of **Alison**'s *hooded head.*

'S more like it.

Pause.

Alison   Dad?

Howard *is fishing in his coat pocket.*

Howard   Yes, love?

Alison   Why am I wearing the hood?

Howard   So I can't see your face.

He pulls a revolver from his pocket and shoots **Alison** *in the head – the retort startling.* **Alison**'s *head is jerked forward by the shot. She slumps to the ground.* **Howard** *stoops down and pulls the hood off his daughter's head. Pause. He walks away as the moon and the photograph fade.*

On the screen the words 'Four Weeks Ago. Monday' appear. **Dr Meyers** *is revealed sitting near* **Alison**. *She is smoking.*

Dr Meyers   That's it?

Alison *stands up.*

Alison   That's it.

Dr Meyers (*pause*)   So, how'd the dream make you feel?

Alison   How'd it make me feel?

Dr Meyers   Yes.

Alison   How did my dad shooting me and burying me in the woods for a birthday present make me feel?

Dr Meyers   Yes.

Alison   Well . . . I was disappointed, obviously. I'd asked for a bike.

Dr Meyers *glances at her watch. Beat.*

Alison   There was a girl killed a couple of weeks ago, in some woods. It's stuck in my head. I keep thinking about her . . . that's probably why I had the dream.

Dr Meyers   And how is your relationship with your father?

Alison   Good. Fine. It's . . . it's . . . We don't talk much.

Dr Meyers   Uhuh. Well . . . there's some more background stuff I . . . Now, Alison, you work don't you?

Alison *takes her coat off.*

Alison   Yes.

Dr Meyers   At . . . (*Reading.*) Telco?

Alison   Uhuh.

Dr Meyers   And what do you do there?

Alison   I talk to wankers.

Dr Meyers   Therapist?

Alison   Adult chatline

Dr Meyers   Ah. And how is that?

Alison (*beat*)   There are a lot of strange people out there.

Dr Meyers   Yup

Alison   Not just the callers. They're . . . you know. But, I mean the people who run the place. It's very weird. At first they monitor your calls, but I think they get so bored they just leave you alone after a while You're supposed to stick to these scripts but . . . well, to be honest, just my opinion, the quality of writing isn't that great. And *I* think if you ad-lib a little it gives it a . . . a . . .

Dr Meyer   Spontaneity.

Alison   A spontaneity. yes. (*Beat.*) They think I'm an idiot.

Dr Meyers   Who does?

Alison   Everyone at work.

Dr Meyers   And what makes you think that everyone at work thinks you're an idiot?

Alison   They told me. They had this vote on it. (*Beat.*) You know what they make you do if you mess fall below your target?

Dr Meyers   What?

Alison   They make you stand on your desk. Really. The Supervisor walks past and tells you to get on your desk and you just have stand there. Nobody even bothers to look at you.

Dr Meyers   Uhuh. Well . . . that sounds very stressful.

Alison   Yeah, well . . . I'm gonna leave. I went to the university today, see about enrolling, so . . . (*Pause.*) I . . . I've started doing this thing. I pretend to be other people. I mean, outside work even. I meet some man and I make up this thing of who I am, like a . . . like a little film.

Dr Meyers   And these people that you pretend to be . . . do they have anything in common?

Alison   Yes. They all have problems. I mean . . . it's sort of pathetic, isn't it? That's my problem. I pretend to be people with problems.

Dr Meyers   What about when they find out who you really are?

Alison   I finish it before they do. It's amazing. You tell a man you've got some serious problem and you don't see them for dust. (*Beat.*) I ring my dad sometimes. He's a Samaritan and I ring him and pretend to be someone with . . . you know, cancer of the head, or, or my brother's shagging me. (*Beat.*) Maybe I just want some attention.

A phone rings.

Dr Meyers   I'm sorry . . . I need to . . .

She answers the phone.

Dr Meyers. (*Beat.*) Yes, there is a problem. The problem is that I asked for . . . I specifically asked for the blue and red panes to form a checkerboard effect across the top row. (*Beat.*) No. The top row. (*Beat.*) I don't know . . . the, the ugly one . . . with the ginger hair. Yes. Jim. Well, that isn't my problem, is it? (*Beat.*) Well, I'm not paying you until it's put right. Then get this Jim person to ring me!

She hangs up and buries her face in her hands.

They are driving me . . .

She looks up again.

Do you have a conservatory?

Alison   Not on me.

Dr Meyers   Well, should you ever decide to get a conservatory, do not use T. Allen and Co.

She lights another cigarette.

Sorry. Where . . . do you want to sit down?

Alison   No. Thanks.

Dr Meyers   Okay. Where were we?

Alison   Trying to get someone's attention.

Dr Meyers   Yes. Right. Pretending to be different people. Why do you think you do that?

Alison *considers.*

Alison   I'm mentally ill.

Dr Meyers   Uhuh. (*Beat.*) Would you say you had a very religious upbringing?

Alison (*beat*)   Yes. I suppose so.

Dr Meyers   And what about now?

Alison   Now? Now I don't believe in God any more.

Dr Meyers   Right. And what would you say caused this
. . . this loss of faith in God?

Alison   He rang me at work

Dr Meyers   God?

Alison   Dad. (*Beat.*) I mean, he didn't know it was me . . .
He hung up, after a bit. I think he felt guilty or . . . I don't
know whether I would have kept going or not. (*Beat.*) He's
very lonely.

The phone rings again.

Dr Meyers   Sorry. I won't . . .

She answers.

Dr Meyers. Who are you? Who? No, I don't . . . I . . . I want
to speak to someone called Jim. Well, then could you get
him, please? (*Without looking up.*) This is . . . they are driving
me . . .

Alison *climbs on to the table and stands there.* **Dr Meyer** *doesn't
notice.*

Is this Jim? Are you the ugly one?

A beat begins. **Ruth** *appears handcuffed by one wrist to the chair she
is sitting upon.* **George** *stands in front of her. On the screen the
words 'One Year Ago' appear.* **George** *is searching through her
handbag. He takes out her purse and searches through it. He takes some
money out.*

George   Where's the rest of it?

Ruth (*flatly*)   That's all I've got.

George   Where's the rest of your fucking money, tart?

Ruth   That's all I've got.

George (*beat*)   Then you're going to have to give me
something else.

He moves closer towards her.

Ruth (*flatly*)   My car keys are there. You could take the . . .

George   Open your legs. (*Beat.*) Open your legs or I'm . . .

He stares off to one side suddenly.

Pause.

Ruth   What?

George   Nothing, I just . . . it's nothing.

Ruth   What?

George   I just . . . (*Beat.*) I didn't leave any water for him.

Ruth (*beat*)   What?

George   It's . . . I didn't put any fresh water out and he'd nearly finished the . . .

Ruth   Will you forget about the dog, George? WILL YOU FORGET ABOUT THE FUCKING DOG!!

George   DON'T SHOUT AT ME! (*Beat.*) Okay. Okay. Open your . . . open your legs.

Ruth   This is ridiculous. I knew this was . . . I feel . . . I feel ridiculous.

George   I just . . . Let's start again. Let's . . . let's start again. Open your legs.

Ruth   I wanna go home.

George   God's sake! You said you'd try!

Ruth   I have tried, George. I have tried all of your stupid games. But believe it or not, being mugged by a moron is not my idea of an erotic fantasy.

George (*quietly*)   Don't call me a moron!

Ruth   Take this off me. (*Beat.*) George? Take the handcuffs off me.

George (*beat*)   No.

Ruth (*beat. Softly*)   Take the handcuffs off me now.

George (*faltering*)   You don't give the orders here . . . tart.

Ruth *kicks him hard in the shin.*

George (*holding his leg*)   Jesus, Ruth! What did you do that for?

Ruth   Happy Anniversary.

Ruth *stands up and begins to walk away ,dragging the chair with her.*

George   Ruth? Where are you going? You can't take the chair! That's the hotel's chair!

*We hear the long queal of tyres as a car skids out of control. Lights cut. We hear the sound of car crashing. Rise on **Ruth** and **Morris** sitting by the roadside. **Ruth** has a coat wrapped around her. In front of them a small object lies underneath **Morris**'s coat. On the screen the words 'Ten Weeks Ago' appear. They stare at the bundle.*

Ruth   He had this way of looking at me. I know it sounds . . . but it was just like the way my mother looked at me. It was like he saw you very clearly and didn't think much of you, you know? And then he would turn away and pant. It was so . . . it was just full of contempt. (*Beat.*) He was looking at me like that. I could feel him doing it and it was making me so angry . . . I think that's why I didn't see the bend.

Morris   Do you want some chocolate? For the sugar? I've got a Mars Bar.

Ruth   No, thank you. I'm sorry if he gets blood on your coat.

Morris   That's all right. (*Beat.*) He wouldn't have felt anything.

Ruth   You think so?

Morris   He wouldn't have felt a thing. I mean the windscreen maybe, and the, the tree but that was . . . that was in seconds so . . .

She looks at him as if seeing him for the first time.

Ruth   What are you doing here, Morris?

Morris   I was just driving past . . . I didn't see it happen.

Ruth stares at the bundle under the coat.

Ruth   Did he just move?

Morris gets us and peers under the coat.

Morris   I wouldn't have thought so.

He sits beside her again.

Ruth (*beat*)   This has been a very *strange* week. (*Beat.*) Yesterday . . . I . . . I'd had a row with my husband and I went to a book shop and I . . . I was thinking about your film and the Waitress and . . . I stole a book.

Morris (*beat*)   What book did you steal?

Ruth   *Motorcycle Maintenance*. (*Beat.*) I don't have a motorbike. (*Beat.*) We've got a Volvo V70 Estate. (*Beat.*) You know what?

Morris   What?

Ruth   It felt good.

Morris takes out his cigarette case.

Gun Crazy. (*Beat.*) Can I have one?

He lights two cigarettes and gives her one. Pause.

I'm shaking

Morris   Close your eyes.

She does so.

Now breathe in through your nose and out through your mouth.

She does so.

Now let your mind grow still. Don't hold on to thoughts, don't push them away. Just let them pass. (*Beat.*) Rest your hands in your lap.

Still with her eyes closed, she reaches out and touches his groin. Pause.

That's my lap.

Ruth   Would you like to have sex?

Morris (*beat*)   No.

Ruth   Right.

Pause. She keeps her hand there.

Morris   I can't have sex.

Ruth   Right. Is that a physical thing?

Morris   No. It's a spiritual thing. I want to focus all my energy on the plan.

Ruth   Right.

She takes her hand away. Pause.

I think I will have that Mars Bar.

He passes it to her. He sits meditating while she eats. A siren approaches. It grows in volume and then cuts. Lights up on **Ray**. *He faces his* **Supervisor** *– a younger man, who is reading from a sheet of paper. On the screen the word 'Yesterday' appears.*

Security Supervisor   'Four weeks ago . . . phoned in sick for afternoon shift, three weeks ago . . . hour and a half late for afternoon shift, last week . . . phoned in sick again, this week . . . complaint about inappropriate comment made to female customer, complaint about abusive behaviour to gentlemen in wheelchair . . .'

Ray   All right. First off – that last one, I wasn't abusive, I was firm. And if he thinks he's getting special treatment on account of having little legs, then he's picked the wrong Security Operative, because you know, they're all suspects

to me. But, what I would like to know is where all this
information is coming from?

Security Supervisor   Ray . . .

Ray   Because if this is that Allen coming running to you, I
think you should be aware that he is waging a homosexual
vendetta against me at the moment.

Security Supervisor   What?

Ray   I didn't want to say anything, because I don't, you
know, tittle-tattle, but a while back Allen made a pass at me
which I found disgusting and rejected and ever since then I
believe he has been running a whispering capaign against
me.

Security Supervisor   Ray . . .

Ray   Someone like that is very destructive in a unit. I've
seen it happen in combat situations and it's best just to root
them out and . . .

Security Supervisor   You haven't been in a combat
situation, Ray. You haven't been in the army. And I want
you out of here today.

Ray   All right. I didn't want this becoming a slanging
match but I will say this . . . You sit here, behind your desk
and you have no idea what we're facing out there. They're
animals out there and if I don't have your support in here
then I've got no alternative but to hand me badge in . . .

Security Supervisor   You don't have a badge, Ray, and
if you did you couldn't hand it in because I've just fucking
sacked you!

Ray   Well, you're too late, because I resign.

Security Supervisor   You can't resign, you prick! I've
already sacked you!

Ray   Well, I'm sorry, but I resign.

Security Supervisor (*beat*)   Just get out.

Ray (*quietly*)   I know where you live.

Security Supervisor (*beat*)   No, you don't.

Ray (*beat*)   Well, I could find out.

Lights up on **Alison** *sitting next to a phone in a small grey cubicle. There is a desk lamp glowing faintly beside her. On the screen the words 'Two Weeks Ago' appear. Her phone rings. She answers.*

Alison (*throaty voice*)   Hello. You're through to Adult Fantasy Line. Calls are charged at two ninety-nine a minute. I'm Carla. Who are you?

Lights up on George sitting in his living room, talking into the phone.

George (*beat*)   George.

Alison   Ummm. George. That's a sexy name . . . I bet you're a very sexy man. Shall I tell you what I look like, George?

George   Uh . . .

Alison   Well, I'm a tall, curvy brunette and I'm wearing a silk teddy and stockings.

She stares off, thinking.

I've got . . . I've got this look in my eyes. Something haunted, something mysterious. One of my front teeth is missing. An accident? A mute witness to a violent act? I never explain. Over the teddy I wear a U.S.S.R. military great coat. It's long enough to cover the slight limp I have as a result of childhood polio . . .

George (*distressed*)   Oh, God . . .

Alison (*beat*)   George? Are you all right there, George?

George   I shouldn't . . . Oh God, what am I doing? I'm sorry, Carla . . .

Alison (*beat*)   That's all right, George.

George   No, I'm sorry. I don't want this. This is . . .

Alison Well, that's all right. What *do* you want? (*Beat.*) George? (*Beat.*) Do you want to hang up? (*Beat.*) Do you want to talk?

George I don't know. No. No, what would be the point in . . . My wife's having an affair.

Alison Oh. Oh, I'm sorry George.

George Yes. I think it's someone at work. Some . . . Egg-Head.

Alison I'm really sorry.

George Some, you know, Professor of, of, you know, Latin American Pottery or . . . and meanwhile *I'm* the Moron. She seems to forget that I happen to be running a successful electrical goods retail business, which, you know, in the current climate . . . I mean, that's something a Moron could do, isn't it? I don't think so.

Alison That sounds very painful.

George (*becoming upset*) I'm sorry. You don't want to hear this. It's pathetic.

Alison It's fine. You . . . if you want to talk . . .

George No, it's just . . . it's . . . well, in the bedroom area . . . for example. It's . . . I have tried so hard. You wouldn't believe . . . massages and candles, I got a vibrating bed and, and I thought . . . food, you know? I put some ice cream on her . . . *down there* . . . and so I'm, you know, giving her oral pleasure and I look up and she's got the tub, eating the rest of it. It's, it's humiliating you know. She wasn't even hungry, we'd just eaten. It was just . . . *cruel.*

Alison You could leave her, George.

George I know. It's what I should . . . but I'm not . . . I'm not good at being alone.

Alison You can be with someone else and still be alone.

George (*upset*)   No, I couldn't . . . being in the house with no one. Eric's gone now. I couldn't . . . I couldn't . . .

Alison   George? George, you have to . . . be strong George. You can't just beg someone to love you. Make her love you, George . . .

George   I've tried! Aromatherapy and, and . . .

Alison   I'm not talking about aromatherapy. She wants excitement? Be *exciting*. Be an *adventurer*. Be . . .

George   Back-packing?

Alison   No, not . . . I'm talking about *you*. She doesn't know the real you. You don't know the real you. There is nothing more exciting for a woman than the Stranger.

George   The Stranger.

Alison   The Stranger.

George   Be strange. Yes. That's . . . I can be strange.

Alison   The Stranger.

George   Yes. Stranger. (*Beat.*) Thank you. Thank you for listening. Really.

Alison   That's all right.

George   You get so lonely.

Alison   I know.

George   It's really very kind and . . . how much, how much was it a minute?

Alison   Two ninety-nine.

George   Well, it was very . . . (*Beat, he coughs. Beat.*) So . . . what are you wearing again?

Man's voice (*on telephone*)   Women tell you it's what inside that matters, right?

Lights cut and rise on **Howard** *in his Samaritans cubicle, on the phone. He is extremely tense. On the screen the words 'Three Days Ago' appear.*

Man's voice   Like, they say it's not about the way you look? They're always saying it's a man's personality or, or sense of humour that they find attractive. Well, you know what that is? That's a *lie*. I've got a great personality and I'm always telling jokes and I've never had sex. Never!.

Howard   Simon . . .

Man's voice   Steven.

Howard   Steven . . . do you have a problem you want to discuss?

Man's voice   'S what I'm telling you. I'm telling you the problem.

Howard   No, that's not a problem, Steven. What you're talking about is just some teenage crap.

Man's voice   Hey! You're a Samaritan right? You're supposed to listen to my problem . . .

Howard   It isn't a problem! You want a problem? I can give you a problem! I've got problems you wouldn't believe, so do me a favour and just . . . just fuck off.

He hangs up. Beat. He looks around to see if anyone is watching him. Lights cut and rise on **Ruth** *and* **George** *in the Chinese restaurant.* **Ruth** *has blonde hair. On the screen the words 'Two Weeks Ago' appear.* **George** *finishes eating noisily as he talks.* **Ruth** *stares at her plate.*

George   I'm just saying, big deal, you know? I'm entitled to my opinion. Big deal.

Ruth   Big deal.

George   Big deal. Like three hours and he gets rich and then he dies alone and . . . you know . . . it was like a soap.

Ruth   It was like a soap.

George   Well, it was. One of the American ones. *Knotts Landing.* Same thing.

Ruth   *Citizen Kane* is like *Knotts Landing.*

George *puts his hand flat on the table and begins to slowly stab the knife into the table between his fingers.*

George   And you keep watching because there's all this big thing about the Rosebud thing and then you never even find out who Rosebud was anyway.

Ruth (*beat. Tightly*)   It was the sledge.

George   What?

Ruth   Rosebud was the name of his sledge.

George   What sledge?

Ruth   In the warehouse. It's the last shot, George. What are you doing?

George   Well, I didn't see it. (*Beat.*) What's a sledge got to do with anything?

Ruth   What are you doing?

George   What?

Ruth   With the knife.

George   This? It's a sailor thing.

Ruth   You're not a sailor. You sell televisions.

George   I've been in the navy.

Ruth   You've been in the navy?

George   Yes.

Ruth   When?

George   When I was younger. (*Beat.*) Fourteen or . . .

Ruth (*beat*)   Fourteen?

George   Yes. Fourteen. Sea . . . Sea Cadets.

Ruth   I didn't know that.

George   You don't know everything about me.

George goes faster.

Ruth   You're gonna hurt yourself.

George   Used to do this all the time. In the . . . mess.

Ruth   Will you . . . *will you stop it!*

She tries to stop him and jolts his arm. He stabs his hand. Pause.

I'm sorry.

George (*in pain*)   'S okay.

Ruth   Are you . . . is it all right?

George   Fine! (*Beat.*) 'S fine. (*Beat.*) I've had worse in my time.

He wraps his hand in the napkin. Pause.

Ruth   Look, let's . . . shall we go?

George   What's the hurry? It's your birthday. We could go dancing or . . .

Ruth   I'm tired.

Morris *appears in his waiter's jacket.*

Morris   Is everything all right?

Ruth *turns away.*

Ruth   Fine. Thank you.

Morris holds out two Fortune Cookies. **George** *takes one and opens it.*

George (*reading*)   'Do not wrestle the Pig. You will both get dirty but the pig will like it.' (*Beat.*) That's . . . what does that mean?

Morris   Madam?

Ruth   Read it for me.

He breaks open the cookie.

Morris (*reading*)   'When the Student is ready, the Master arrives.'

She stares at him.

George   That's not funny either. I thought these were supposed to be jokes?

Ruth   You're thinking of Christmas crackers.

He finishes his drink and stands.

George   Well, if you'd just . . .

*He whispers something to **Morris** who points to someone at the bar.* **George** *leaves. Pause.*

Ruth   What'd did he ask you?

George   He asked me where the manager was.

Ruth   Oh God, he's going to complain about the bill.

Morris *sits in **George***'*s seat.*

Morris   I like your hair. You look very beautiful.

Ruth (*beat*)   He's been drinking. My husband. Eric came back today.

Morris   Eric?

Ruth   The dog. He's had him stuffed. He's put him by the TV in the living room.

She reaches forward and brushes the hair off his forehead.

You've got a . . . you've got a nasty bruise on your forehead there.

Morris   Uh, yes. (*Beat.*) I was beaten up yesterday.

Ruth   Oh my God . . . Who did it?

Morris   A security guard in a shop. I stole a dress and he caught me and beat me up.

Ruth (*pause*)   You . . . you stole a dress? Why would you steal a dress?

Morris pulls a bag out from under his jacket and gives it to Ruth.

Morris   Happy birthday.

Beat. Ruth opens the bag and takes out an identical dress to the one Morris had stolen.

I saw you were booked in for the birthday deal . . . I thought I'd get you something.

Ruth (*beat*)   You stole this dress for me?

Morris (*beat*)   Actually, no. Not that one. The man who beat me up took the one I'd stolen off me. I bought that one in Bainbridges. (*Beat.*) There's a lot of hostility out there, isn't there?

Ruth   You . . . Why did you try and steal it?

Morris   I thought you'd like it more that way. (*Beat.*) *Gun Crazy*?

Ruth stares at him.

Ruth (*quietly*)   Why are you doing this to me? Is this . . . is this a game to you?

Morris   What am I doing?

Ruth   You . . . I make a . . . I throw myself at you and you . . . I make an *idiot* of myself and I think, all right, you don't . . . you don't find me attractive and that's fine and now . . . you do . . . you do *this* for me and I don't know what . . . (*Beat.*) Do you *want* me?

Pause.

Morris   Do you like the dress?

Beat. Ruth stands up and leaves. Beat. Unperturbed, Morris examines the food in front of him. He starts to eat. A sudden clash of cymbals. A Chinese Dragon appears and dances frenetically around the table. It stops and George pops out from under the head. He stares at Morris, his grin fading.

George (*calmly*)   Are you finished here, sir?

Lights cut. A spot snaps on to **Ray**, *facing the audience. His head is shaved. On the screen the word 'Today' appears.*

Ray   All the time, people have been thinking I was an idiot. I know they have. Always been like that. But now . . . now this has become something really big. I went to the university but they said Ruth had quit. He's got her. I know he has. And I know what I've got to do. My whole life has pointed in one direction. I see that now. (*Beat.*) RUTH!!

Telco. **Ray** *strides past* **Alison**'s *cubicle, then spots her hiding under the table and comes back.*

Ruth! Come on! We're going!

Alison   What are you doing here, Dave? How did you know I was here?

Ray *begins to drag her out.*

Ray   Come on!

Alison   GET OFF ME! I WORK HERE!

Ray   What are you doing? WHAT ARE YOU DOING? Fucking porn lines? It's disgusting! (*Beat.*) Is he making you do this?

Alison   What?

Ray   Lang! Is he making you do this?

Alison   All right, listen to me, Dave! I'm not Ruth! I made it up! My name's Alison! Everything I told you was a lie. It was a game . . . it was just a stupid game!

A **Supervisor** *appears.*

Supervisor   What the . . . what's going on?

Ray (*to* **Alison**)   You don't have to be afraid of him, Ruth. You can come with me.

Supervisor   Right. I want you out of here.

Ray (*in her face*)   FUCK OFF! NOW!

Frightened, the **Supervisor** *leaves.*

Alison   I made it all up!

Ray   I checked your story! There was a girl killed in some woods a couple of weeks ago. You were right, Ruth!

Alison   Will you please just go?

Ray   What did he do to you? Is it drugs?

Alison   What?

He grabs her arm roughly, checking for tracks.

Ray   Whatever he's said, right? Whatever he's threatened you with, you don't have to be afraid. I'm getting you out of this.

Alison   WILL YOU FUCK OFF, YOU MADMAN!

The **Supervisor** *returns with a* **Man**.

Man   All right, sir. I want you to leave now. The police are on their way.

He goes to shove **Ray** *who instantly adopts a martial arts pose.*

Ray   Back off! Back off! You don't wanna know what I'll do. You don't wanna fucking know what I'll do! Ruth! Listen to me! I'm not really a dentist!

Man   Just leave now or you're going to be arrested.

Ray *backs away. A low drone begins.*

Ray (*as he goes*)   I know what's going on here! I'll get him, Ruth. I swear to you. I'll get Lang!

Alison *begins to cry. The drone builds. On the screen we see the horserace in slow motion. The word 'Today' appears. The casino. The drone builds to a crescendo and cuts. Underneath we hear a muzak version of 'Twenty-four Hours from Tulsa' by Gene Pitney.*
Howard *is at the roulette table next to the* **Gambler**. *The same* **Croupier** *hands him a stack of chips.*

Croupier   One thousand.

Howard *pulls the chips towards a pile he already has.*

Gambler   Definitely your night.

Howard   It's not enough. It's nowhere near enough.

Gambler   Well, it never is, is it?

Croupier   Place your bets.

Howard   What's the maximum bet on a number?

Croupier   Five hundred.

Howard   Five hundred? Thirty five to one . . .

He counts his chip stacks.

Gambler   Big night, is it?

Howard *stares at him, white faced.*

Howard   I sold my wife's wedding ring for the money.

Gambler   Yeah? You'd better win, hadn't you, or she's not gonna be happy.

Howard (*beat*)   Yes. (*Beat.*) How old are you?

Gambler   What?

Howard   I need a number. I need, I need a sign, you know?

Gambler (*beat*)   Can I give you a bit of advice? If you can't lose . . . don't play.

Howard   I can't lose. And I have to play. That's . . . that's my life now. I can't lose and I have to play. (*Beat. Suddenly.*) What song is this?

Gambler   What?

Howard   The song! Gene Pitney. Tulsa . . . something from Tulsa?

Gambler   Twenty-four hours.

Howard   Yes. (*To* **Croupier**.) What colour's twenty-four?

Croupier   Noir.

Howard   Yes. That's . . . yes.

He passes her a stack of chips.

Croupier   Five hundred on twenty-four noir.

She spins the wheel. The horserace freezes on the screen. The drone builds again, drowning out the muzak. **Howard** *and the* **Gambler** *stare intently.*

Croupier   No more bets . . .

Lights and music cut. **Ruth** *sits reading, a standard lamp beside her. A stuffed dog sits nearby. She stares at the dog, then back at her book.* **George** *appears, holding the dress that* **Morris** *bought. He stands beside her, looking down.*

George   What are you reading?

Ruth (*without looking up*)   *Motorcycle Maintenance.*

George (*beat*)   Right. (*Beat.*) Why did you marry me, Ruth?

Ruth   You didn't smoke.

Pause.

George   Who's Bart Tare?

Ruth   *Gun Crazy.*

George   What?

Ruth (*still reading*)   He's a character in a film called *Gun Crazy*. Why?

George *drops the dress into her lap.*

George (*beat*)   He sent you this today.

Pause. **Ruth** *stares at the dress.* **George** *holds up a card.*

'I'm sorry. Bart Tare.' (*Beat.*) Who is he?

Beat. **Ruth** *holds up the dress.*

Ruth   I don't know, but I'd say he was a size eight.

George   Why's he sorry?

Ruth   You're in my light. I'm halfway through changing the spark plugs . . .

He takes the book from her.

George   I want to know who he is.

Ruth   He's no one.

George   Are you . . . are you two . . . you know?

Ruth   Are we two what? The word is sex. Why do you never say it, George? The word is sex, or fucking or screwing or . . . there are thousands of words, George . . .

George (*beat*)   I was going to say are you two in love? (*Pause.*) Are you?

Ruth   Don't be stupid.

George   DON'T CALL ME STUPID! YOU WILL NOT CALL ME STUPID!

Pause.

I'm . . . Sorry. I'm . . . I'm very . . . work and everything. Things are very . . . I'm stressed. (*Beat.*) I should never have gotten into retail. (*Beat.*) I think you should know . . .

Ruth (*gently*)   George . . .

George   I think you should know before you make any decisions that you might regret that . . .

Ruth   George . . .

George   . . . that I am a man capable of change. I intend to complete re-think my fashion decisions and general appearance and sell the business and use the profits to . . . to . . . fund a new life for us both . . .

Ruth   I think I should leave, George.

George   . . . in, in, in Hotel Management. (*Beat.*) For example.

Ruth   It isn't you. It's me.

George (*beat*)   I know that. I know that! (*Beat.*) Go on then. Off you go.

Ruth   George . . .

George   What? George what? Did you think I was going to break down in tears? Start wailing? I'm not the crying type, Ruth.

She starts to leave.

Just one question. This man of yours . . . does he pull in a thirty-three per cent profit per annum? (*Beat.*) No? Does he . . . does he regularly holiday in the Southern Hemisphere? Does he buy you a Tiffany pearl necklace? No? Well, then enlighten me, Ruth. Just what does he have that I don't?

Ruth   He has an unusually large penis.

George breaks down. Ruth hurries to him and hugs him.

George! It's . . . Shh . . . George it's not that. It's nothing to do with that. I'm just being cruel and that's . . . that's why I've got to go because staying here is making me cruel and I'm not cruel, George! I'm really not! I'm just unhappy.

He pulls away, wiping his face.

George   I'm unhappy. But I wouldn't have left you.

Pause. She picks up the dress.

Ruth   Goodbye, George.

She hesitates, then moves to pat the stuffed dog.

George (*hissing*)   Don't you touch Eric! (*Beat.*) Not one hair on his head.

Ruth goes to leave.

I would have grown a beard for you.

Ruth (*beat*)   I know you would.

She leaves. We hear the dull roar of a metro train building. **George** *looks up at the standard lamp. He smashes it to one side. The light goes out. The roar builds. Lights up on metro train carriage.* **Ruth** *sits in her coat, the dress folded on her lap.* **Howard** *sits beside her, his briefcase beside him. Further along the seats sits another passenger reading a newspaper.* **Howard** *drums his hands on his knees, a little drunk, unable to contain his elation.*

Howard (*suddenly*)   Can I ask you something?

Ruth   What?

Howard   Can I ask you something? Have you found God?

Ruth (*staring straight ahead*)   No. Have you lost him?

Howard   Well . . . I know you're just joking, but in a funny way, I had lost him. But you know what? God hadn't lost me. I don't mean to bother you but something happened to me tonight. Something incredible. Do you . . . do you believe in signs?

Ruth *ignores him.* **Howard** *turns to the other passenger.*

Sir? Do you believe in signs?

Passenger   What?

Howard *stands up, excited.*

Howard   Signs. Messages from . . . a sense of a force
that's working through us all. I know what you're thinking
. . . there's no sense in this world . . . it's just . . . meaningless.
God help me, I was beginning to think like that too but . . .
tonight I received a sign and it was, it was so clear, it was
. . . I was saved. Tonight. Right here in this city. God spoke
to me. And he said there is a meaning. And you are not
alone.

He crosses to the **Passenger**.

I love you.

Passenger   What?

Howard   This is the meaning. This is why we're here. To
love each other. And, and I want you to know that I love
you.

Passenger   Well . . . this is all so sudden.

Howard   I know. You're joking. Isn't it strange that it's so
hard to hear you're loved? (*Beat.*) Can I sing something for
you?

Passenger   Oh, for fuck's sake . . .

Howard (*singing*)
   Where are those happy days?

He continues the verse.

As **Howard** *sings, the metro stops.* **Ruth** *gets up to leave. She
hesitates, then comes back and picks up* **Howard**'s *briefcase. She gets
off the train.* **Howard** *is still singing as the roar of the train builds
once more, drowning him out. Lights cut. The roar of the train merges
with a rumble of thunder. A flash of lighting. Lights rise on the
Reverend* **Lang** *in his chair.* **Howard** *kneels beside him. Pause.*

Lang   You don't have it?

Howard (*flatly*)   I had it. And then . . . I lost it.

Lang   You lost twenty thousand pounds?

Howard I think someone . . . (*Beat.*) It doesn't matter.

Lang It doesn't matter.

Howard It doesn't matter. I misread the sign. I thought
. . . I thought that was the sign. I thought the money was the
sign. But the money wasn't the sign. This is the sign. (*Beat.*)
The funny thing is . . . I'm glad.

Lang You're glad.

Howard I'm . . . I'm relieved. I've been so tired. I feel . . .
I feel clear now.

Lang (*beat*) Well . . . I'm glad you're clear now, Howard.
Meanwhile, I'm out twenty thousand pounds, you miserable
little cunt. (*Beat.*) Do you know what this is going to do? Do
you know what the publicity is going to do to us?

Howard I want to be punished. I sold Helen's wedding
ring. I want to be punished.

Lang That's good, because I'm going to see to it that you
are punished, Howard. I'm going to see to it that you go to
prison, and if it's at all possible I'm going to see to it that
you have your arse fucked until it resembles a Japanese flag.
(*Pause.*) You think you understand God's signs, Howard?
You don't understand anything. You don't understand
anything.

He goes to a phone and lifts it to dial. There is a flash of lightning.
Ray *appears.*

Ray Put the phone down.

Lang *stares at him. He puts the phone back.*

Ray Mr Lang? Mr Philip Lang?

Lang Who are you? What are you doing here?

Ray What money are you two talking about, then? Drug
money? Porn money? Blood money?

Lang How did you get in here?

Ray   Did you think I wouldn't find you? Did you really think I . . . you're in the phone book. (*Beat.*) YOU'RE IN THE FUCKING PHONE BOOK!

Lang *looks at* **Howard**.

Lang (*to* **Howard**)   Is this . . . do you think you can scare me, Howard? You think you can intimidate me?

Howard   This is nothing to do with . . . I've never seen him before!

Lang   Big mistake, Howard! Big fucking mistake!

Ray   Look at me, Lang. Look at me.

Lang *looks at him.*

Ray   Where's Ruth?

Lang   Who?

Ray   I want Ruth. And I want that photograph.

Lang   What . . . what are you talking about?

Ray   I'm talking about a murdered girl, Lang. I'm talking about Eve. I'm talking about the photograph you took of her after you'd killed her.

Lang   What the fuck are you . . . ?

Ray   WHERE IS RUTH?

Lang   All right. Now, now that's . . . I want you out of my house, right now!

He walks towards **Ray**.

Ray   Well then, maybe you'd like to meet my friend here.

He draws the Taser. **Lang** *stops.*

Ray   Nineteen thirty-three. Victor Appleton writes *Tom Swift in the Land of Wonders* – one in a series of children's books . . .

Lang *punches him.* **Ray** *staggers backwards, loses his balance and crashes to the floor.* **Lang** *kicks him viciously. He turns to* **Howard** *who is still kneeling.*

Lang   BIG FUCKING MISTAKE, HOWARD! You think I wouldn't be a fighter? Man of God? Men of God are fighters, Howard! We've got something to fight for!

He kicks **Ray** *again.*

Fighting for the light!

He kicks **Ray** *again.*

Fighting 'gainst the darkness!

He goes to kick **Ray** *again but* **Ray** *grabs his leg and with his other hand pushes the Taser into* **Lang**'s *groin. There is a flash of sparks.* **Lang** *is flung back on to the floor by the shock. He lies convulsing.* **Ray** *struggles to his feet.* **Lang** *is still.* **Howard** *and* **Ray** *stare at him.* **Ray** *approaches him cautiously and checks his pulse. He stands up again. He coughs. Pause.*

Ray   Right.

He walks quickly away. Pause. **Howard** *stares at* **Lang**'s *body. He stares up at the ceiling. A flash of lightning. Thunder rumbles. Lights cut.*

A garden. Night. **George** *kneels beside the stuffed dog, screwing a small plate back into place behind the dog's head. He has been drinking from a bottle of whisky and has a tool box beside him.* **Ray** *approaches.*

Ray   What the fuck are you doing out here? I've been knocking at the front door.

George *(drunk)*   Wait. I'm . . . I'm nearly done.

Ray   George, listen . . . something's happened.

George   WAIT!

Pause. He finishes.

Right. Are you ready?

Ray   What for?

George *flicks a switch and the dog's eyes light up.* **George** *stares at it.*

George   What do you think?

Ray   I think . . . it's . . . it's . . .

George (*solemnly*)   I think he looks beautiful. He looks beautiful now. Like an angel or something. He loved the garden.

George *drinks from the bottle.*

Ray   Where is she, George? Where's Ruth?

George   She's left me.

Ray   Where'd she go though, George? (*Beat.*) George! Where's she gone?

George   I don't know. You tell me, Ray. You're the one following her. You're The Shadow.

Ray   Listen to me. She's in danger. She was . . . she was mixed up with someone. Bloke called Lang. I've taken care of him but . . . there's probably others. People working for him. They might have her.

Pause. **George** *stands up.*

George   Why didn't you tell me?

Ray   What?

George   If you knew she was mixed up with someone. You were watching her for me. Why didn't you tell me?

Ray   Because . . . because this was serious stuff! What could someone like you do?

George   Someone like me?

Ray   George! We haven't got time for this! I've gotta find her!

George   Someone like me? A moron, you mean? A dickless moron?

Ray   Fuck this.

He turns to leave. **George** *grabs him by the shirt. It tears open, revealing the tattoo. Pause. A rumble of thunder.*

George   What's that?

Ray (*beat*)   What?

George   Ruth. You've got 'Ruth' tattooed across your chest.

Ray (*beat*)   Where?

George *lets him go.*

George   Oh, Jesus.

Ray   All right. It's not what you think.

George   Oh, Jesus. I feel sick. How could . . . we were friends, Ray.

Ray   This isn't . . . we didn't know each that well . . . but this isn't . . . .

George   I'm a moron. I'm . . . You bought her the dress.

Ray   I didn't exactly buy it . . .

George   Did you fuck her?

Ray   This isn't important now, George.

George   DID YOU FUCK HER!

Ray   NO! (*Beat.*) It isn't . . . it isn't like that. It's . . . it's . . . romance . . . it's special. (*Beat.*) I felt her tits a bit. That's all.

George (*beat*)   Why you? Why would she want you?

Ray   What can I tell you? The danger. The glamour . . .

George *stoops down, comes up with the whiskey bottle and smashes it into* **Ray**'s *face.* **Ray** *falls beside the dog.*

Ray JESUS! FUCKING . . . JESUS!

He lies holding his face. **George** *grabs an aerosol can from the toolbox and sprays it into* **Ray***'s eyes.* **Ray** *yells with pain.* **George** *lets him go and sits down. It begins to rain.* **Ray** *struggles up, holding on to the dog. His face is a mask of blood. He sits breathing heavily.*

Ray All right. All right. I deserved that. But . . . we've got to find her, George. I don't know what they'll do to her! (*Beat.*) George! Will you . . . you've got to help me! (*Beat.*) Fuck . . . I can't . . . I can't see. George! You've gotta . . . I can't fucking see! I can't see!

The rain falls on them for a moment, the dog's eyes glowing in the gloom. We hear **Howard***'s voice.*

Howard's voice . . . I don't know. I don't understand what He wants any more. So that's it. That's everything. I'm sorry.

Light's rise on **Howard** *at home listening to a tape recorder, a microphone in his hand.*

(*On tape.*) I'm sorry for everything.

Howard *stops the tape. He takes out a bottle of pills. Pause. He takes out a coin. He tosses the coin and stares at it. Pause.* **Howard** *pours the pills into his hand. He stares at them. He dials the phone next to him with his free hand. We hear the other end ringing.*

Man's voice Hello, Samaritans.

Howard (*beat*) Hello, Jeff?

Man's voice Yeah.

Howard It's Howard. (*Beat.*) I won't be in tonight.

Man's voice Okay. Are you all right Howard?

Howard (*beat*) Uh, yeah. I'm fine. Bye.

He hangs up. **Alison** *appears behind him, unnoticed.* **Howard** *stares at the pills. He starts to cry.* **Alison** *takes out a mobile phone* *and dials. The phone next to* **Howard** *rings.* **Howard** *stares at it. He picks it up.*

Howard   Hello?

Alison   Dad? It's me. It's Alison.

Howard *turns and stares at her. Lights cut and rise on* **Ruth** *wearing the dress* **Morris** *gave her. She holds* **Howard**'s *briefcase.* **Morris** *sits on his sofa, staring at her. Outside, rain falls.*

Morris   It looks . . . you look . . .

He holds his hands up in a vague gesture.

You've left your husband?

Ruth   Yes.

Morris   Where are you going to go?

Ruth   On a crime spree.

She hands him the briefcase. He opens it and looks inside.

There's about twenty thousand pounds there. It's . . . development money. I want us to develop the film. I want a producer credit. I'm sick of watching things. I want to produce.

Pause.

I need you to say something, Morris. I'm a little . . . I'm sort of improvising here.

Morris   'It's only the first step that is difficult.' (*Beat.*) Kneel on the floor.

She kneels in front of him.

Close your eyes.

She closes her eyes. He walks back to the sofa and sits.

Breathe in through your nose and out through your mouth. (*Beat.*) Now let your mind grow still.

Pause.

Ruth (*eyes closed*)   Read me that passage from the film.

Morris opens the script.

Morris (*reading*)   'But I'm scared. For the first time, I'm really scared, because I'm happy and I love you, and it's too big. It's . . . I want to hide it under a stone, I want to hide this happiness in case people see it, but it's too big, it's like a *Cathedral* and . . . I love you.'

Ruth (*beat*)   Read the last line again.

Morris   'I love you.'

Ruth (*beat*)   And again . . .

Lights cut. A **Waitress** *appears at the extreme stage left, holding a tray with two coffees and a sandwich on it. The diner. A single light bulb is lowered from above, centre stage.*

Waitress   TWENTY-FOUR!

We are in the same diner scene we saw at the beginning of the play – this time seen from the other side of the booth. On the screen the words 'Four Weeks Ago' appear.

TWENTY-FOUR!

The beat cuts.

Ray   . . . Light?

The lone bulb snaps on above the booth. **Morris** *sits by himself.* **Ray** *leans over from the other side of the booth, his hair wet.* **Morris** *takes out a lighter and lights the cigarette* **Ray** *has in his mouth.*

Ray   Ta. Fucking rain, eh?

Morris *smiles.* **Ray** *sits down, disappearing out of sight behind the booth.* **Morris** *studies his menu.*

Waitress (*looking around*)   TWENTY-FOUR!

She disappears into the opposite wings.

(*Offstage.*) TWENTY-FOUR!

Ray's *arm appears.*

Ray (*out of sight*)   Here!

The **Waitress** *stomps back on and disappears behind the booth, depositing the coffees and sandwich at* **Ray** *and* **George**'s *table. She reappears and crosses round to* **Morris**.

Waitress (*staring at her pad*)   What can I get you?

Morris   Just a coffee.

She looks up at him.

Waitress   You've got a fucking nerve.

Morris   Why?

Waitress   Just give me it back.

Morris *hands her the script.*

You prick.

Morris   Why am I a prick?

Waitress   You said you'd read it the next day. That was six fucking weeks ago.

Morris   I'm sorry. I didn't read it the next day. I read it the same night. And then the next day I got on a plane and flew to America.

Waitress   Well, that's very nice for you . . .

Morris   Where I began negotiations to have this film produced.

Pause.

Sit down. Please.

She sits opposite him.

Do you have an agent?

She laughs. He smiles.

Waitress   Okay. That's . . . you brought it back, you read it, you liked it and thanks but . . . you don't have to . . .

Morris   I have certain contacts . . .

Waitress   Please . . . don't give me a *line*, all right?

Morris   . . . people whose opinion count for something and they feel, as I do, that this is a very rare film indeed. Now, I don't believe in putting a price on art but if I *did* believe in that, I would be putting a six figure price on this particular piece of art.

Waitress   Look, this is very funny, but I'm not going to sleep with you.

Behind them, George stands up.

Ray   George . . .

George   I'm going home.

Ray *stands.*

Ray   George, sit down. I'm just . . . I'm just *paraphrasing*, aren't I? Sit down.

They sit again, disappearing.

Morris (*beat*)   I think there's a chance that you are very talented. I know it seems unlikely to you, but I think you should at least consider the possibility.

Waitress   I'm a waitress.

Morris   You don't know what you are yet.

Morris lights a cigarette from his silver case.

You want one?

Beat. She takes one. He lights her cigarette.

Waitress   Nice case.

Morris   Yeah. I got it in an auction. Did you see *Titanic*?

Waitress   The film?

Morris   This is the same case Kate Winslet uses in *Titanic*.

Waitress (*beat*)   I don't have an agent.

Morris   Then I think we should get you one straight away, Mary.

Waitress   That's not my name.

Morris takes the script and looks at the front page.

Morris   Mary Talman?

Waitress   It's a non de plume. Just for writing. (*Beat.*) My name's Eve.

Morris   That's nice. Well, it's gonna be all about you, Eve.

The Polaroid of the girl in the woods fades up on the screen.

We need to talk. What time do you finish?

Pause. She considers. She puts her cigarette out and stands up.

Waitress   I get off at two.

Morris   Fasten your seat belt, it's going to be a bumpy night.

Morris *smiles at her. She walks away. Morris stops smiling. The bulb above him flickers. He stares at it intently. We hear a loud crackling. Morris forms his hand into a gun and aims it at the bulb.*

Morris (*softly*)   Pow.

The bulb goes out, plunging us into darkness as music erupts.

Methuen Drama Contemporary Dramatists
include

Peter Barnes (three volumes)
Sebastian Barry
Edward Bond (six volumes)
Howard Brenton
  (two volumes)
Richard Cameron
Jim Cartwright
Caryl Churchill (two volumes)
Sarah Daniels (two volumes)
Nick Darke
David Edgar (three volumes)
Ben Elton
Dario Fo (two volumes)
Michael Frayn (two volumes)
Paul Godfrey
John Guare
Peter Handke
Jonathan Harvey
Declan Hughes
Terry Johnson (two volumes)
Bernard-Marie Koltès
David Lan
Bryony Lavery
Doug Lucie
David Mamet (three volumes)

Martin McDonagh
Duncan McLean
Anthony Minghella
  (two volumes)
Tom Murphy (four volumes)
Phyllis Nagy
Anthony Nielsen
Philip Osment
Louise Page
Joe Penhall
Stephen Poliakoff
  (three volumes)
Christina Reid
Philip Ridley
Willy Russell
Ntozake Shange
Sam Shepard (two volumes)
Wole Soyinka (two volumes)
David Storey (three volumes)
Sue Townsend
Michel Vinaver (two volumes)
Michael Wilcox
David Wood (two volumes)
Victoria Wood

Methuen Drama Modern Plays
include work by

Jean Anouilh
John Arden
Margaretta D'Arcy
Peter Barnes
Sebastian Barry
Brendan Behan
Dermot Bolger
Edward Bond
Bertolt Brecht
Howard Brenton
Anthony Burgess
Simon Burke
Jim Cartwright
Caryl Churchill
Noël Coward
Lucinda Coxon
Sarah Daniels
Nick Darke
Nick Dear
Shelagh Delaney
David Edgar
David Eldridge
Dario Fo
Michael Frayn
John Godber
Paul Godfrey
David Greig
John Guare
Peter Handke
David Harrower
Jonathan Harvey
Iain Heggie
Declan Hughes
Terry Johnson
Sarah Kane
Charlotte Keatley
Barrie Keeffe
Howard Korder

Robert Lepage
Stephen Lowe
Doug Lucie
Martin McDonagh
John McGrath
Terrence McNally
David Mamet
Patrick Marber
Arthur Miller
Mtwa, Ngema & Simon
Tom Murphy
Phyllis Nagy
Peter Nichols
Joseph O'Connor
Joe Orton
Louise Page
Joe Penhall
Luigi Pirandello
Stephen Poliakoff
Franca Rame
Mark Ravenhill
Philip Ridley
Reginald Rose
David Rudkin
Willy Russell
Jean-Paul Sartre
Sam Shepard
Wole Soyinka
Shelagh Stephenson
C. P. Taylor
Theatre de Complicite
Theatre Workshop
Sue Townsend
Judy Upton
Timberlake Wertenbaker
Roy Williams
Victoria Wood

Methuen Drama World Classics
include

Jean Anouilh (two volumes)
John Arden (two volumes)
Arden & D'Arcy
Brendan Behan
Aphra Behn
Bertolt Brecht (seven volumes)
Büchner
Bulgakov
Calderón
Čapek
Anton Chekhov
Noël Coward (eight volumes)
Eduardo De Filippo
Max Frisch
John Galsworthy
Gogol
Gorky
Harley Granville Barker
  (two volumes)
Henrik Ibsen (six volumes)
Lorca (three volumes)

Marivaux
Mustapha Matura
David Mercer (two volumes)
Arthur Miller (five volumes)
Molière
Musset
Peter Nichols (two volumes)
Clifford Odets
Joe Orton
A. W. Pinero
Luigi Pirandello
Terence Rattigan
  (two volumes)
W. Somerset Maugham
  (two volumes)
August Strindberg
  (three volumes)
J. M. Synge
Ramón del Valle-Inclán
Frank Wedekind
Oscar Wilde

Lightning Source UK Ltd.
Milton Keynes UK

175259UK00004B/4/P